Spatial Correlation and Poverty Prediction Index (PPI) Generation Using Artificial Intelligence

Jenifer Lowan

Contents

Chapter 1

Introduction

This chapter provides an overview of the importance of Poverty Prediction. It delves into the crucial role of Computer Vision (CV), Remote Sensing (RS), and Artificial Intelligence, particularly Deep Learning, in Poverty prediction, as these areas provide an opportunity to utilize multimodal input indicators for more accurate and granular poverty prediction. This chapter introduces the motivation behind the proposed work, the significance of integrating remote sensing data with socioeconomic and environmental variables, and the scope of developing a comprehensive predictive framework. Furthermore, this chapter outlines the scope of the proposed work, as well as the organization of the thesis.

1.1 Brief Description of the Research

Poverty is one of the biggest obstacles to human progress and sustainable development. The United Nations Sustainable Development Goals (SDGs) [1] are a global plan to remove deprivation and ensure that everyone has access to basic needs and opportunities. The aim is that by 2030, all people can live with peace, dignity, and prosperity. Goal 1 of the SDGs focuses on ending poverty in all its forms, showing the world's shared commitment

Figure 1.1: United Nations's 17 Sustainable Development Goals
[2]

to this important cause. Since all 17 SDGs are connected, as shown in Figure 1.1 progress in one area helps to achieve progress in others, leading to overall sustainable growth and development.

India, having a population of billion people and a variety of cultures, languages, and traditions, struggles with varied challenges of poverty. Despite huge economic development in recent decades, a major portion of the population continues to remain poor and face exclusion, reinforcing the need for targeted policies and development strategies for inclusion. Poverty landscape of India reflects its rich variety of social and economic disparities, with rural and urban areas giving distinct challenges and opportunities for poverty alleviation efforts.

Effectively addressing this major challenge of Poverty demands not only sustained alleviation efforts but also the precise identification and targeting of the most affected populations and regions. Accurate poverty measurement is essential for evaluating economic inequality and designing effective policies. Assessments occur ordinally (tracking trends over time and space) or cardinally (quantifying poverty depth to evaluate programs) [3]. Conceptually, poverty measurement rests on two paradigms: the welfarist approach, focused on utility from consumption, and the non-welfarist approach, emphasizing tangible capabilities and outcomes like health and education [4]. Understanding this distinction is vital for developing robust poverty metrics and advancing strategies to eradicate poverty globally the core aim of Sustainable Development Goal 1 (SDG 1).

1.2 What is Poverty

Poverty is a multidimensional phenomenon that reflects the lack of access to basic human needs such as food, shelter, education, healthcare, and economic opportunities. It functions both as a cause and a consequence of inequality, often persisting across generations. Broadly, poverty can be classified into absolute poverty and relative poverty, defined as follows:

- **Absolute Poverty:** Refers to individuals living on less than $3 per day (based on 2021 purchasing power parity), as defined by the World Bank [5]. It represents a fixed threshold below which basic human needs such as food, shelter, and clothing cannot be met.

- **Relative Poverty:** Defined in comparison to a society's average standard of living. According to the United Nations' Multidimensional Poverty Index (MPI) [6], poverty extends beyond income to include deprivations in education, health, and living standards, emphasizing disparities in access to essential services such as clean water, electricity, and sanitation.

1.3 Poverty Prediction in India

Poverty indicators in India includes a wide array of socio-economic dimensions. These indicators include income groups, employment status, access to education and healthcare, housing conditions, nutritional conditions, and gender disparities. Although national averages gives a broad overview of poverty trends, regional variations enforce the importance of context-specific analysis that takes into account local realities and challenges.

Poverty is a complex phenomenon comprising of various deprivation factors, including economic, social, and environmental. To capture the complexity of poverty, a multidimensional approach that includes different aspects of well-being and human development is needed. In this regard, the National Multidimensional Poverty Index (MPI), as presented in NITI Aayog's Progress Review 2023 report, offers a comprehensive framework for measuring and understanding poverty [7].

1.4 Indicators of Poverty

Poverty is assessed across three key dimensions: health, education, and standard of living. Each dimension consists of specific indicators that defines different aspects of deprivation, and their contributions to overall poverty are weighted accordingly. The MPI framework emphasizes the importance of considering multiple dimensions of poverty, recognizing that deprivation is not limited to income-based measures alone.

1. **Health Dimension:** According to the MPI framework, the first dimension of poverty focuses on health and comprises three key indicators Nutrition, Child and Adolescent Mortality, and Maternal Health.

These indicators capture essential aspects of individual well-being, with Nutrition contributing 50% to the health dimension, while Child and Adolescent Mortality and Maternal Health each contribute 25%.

2. **Education Dimension:** The second dimension, education, emphasizes access to quality learning opportunities and includes two indicators Years of Schooling and School Attendance. Both indicators carry equal weight, each contributing 50% to the education dimension.

3. **Standard of Living Dimension:** The third dimension reflects socio-economic living conditions and overall quality of life. It includes seven indicators Cooking Fuel, Sanitation, Drinking Water, Housing, Electricity, Assets, and Bank Account Access. Each indicator contributes equally, accounting for one-seventh of the standard of living dimension [8].

Poverty can be due to weak governance, corruption, and inadequate public services which impacts overall services provided to public. It can be due to climate change, natural disasters, and resource depletion which affect low-income communities. Due to societal impacts of discrimination based on gender, ethnicity, or caste which limits opportunities. Wars and forced displacement destroys livelihoods and infrastructure resulting in local poverty.

Traditional methods of poverty measurement depend on household-based surveys, such as Demographic and Health Surveys (DHS), which involve manually collecting data from individuals. Analyzing such data is often time-consuming, resource-intensive, and costly. In a vast and diverse country like India, conducting these surveys at regular intervals poses significant challenges due to inaccessibility, particularly in remote or conflict-affected regions, where data collection may be extremely difficult or even unfeasible.

1.5 Evolution of Poverty Estimation Methods

1.5.1 Traditional Approaches (Surveys, Census)

Traditional survey and census data form the foundation of poverty mapping, offering comprehensive and representative insights into key socioeconomic indicators. These datasets typically assess poverty across dimensions such as income, education, healthcare access, and sanitation, thereby serving as the empirical basis for generating spatially detailed poverty estimates. However, despite their value, such data sources are often constrained by infrequent updates and susceptibility to sampling and reporting biases, which can limit the timeliness, accuracy, and spatial granularity of the resulting analyses [9].

In response to these limitations, Small Area Estimation (SAE) has gained prominence as a vital statistical methodology for improving spatial resolution in poverty assessment. By enabling the estimation of poverty rates at subnational or micro-geographic levels, SAE employs model-based techniques to generate finely detailed poverty maps. This enhanced granularity provides a deeper understanding of poverty distribution across heterogeneous regions, empowering policymakers with precise, localized insights for designing more effective and targeted interventions [10] [11] [12].

The integration of traditional surveys, census data, and Small Area Estimation (SAE) methods establishes a robust framework for poverty analysis. This combined approach enables the formulation of data-driven strategies for poverty alleviation, ensuring that policy decisions related to resource distribution and program implementation are both empirically grounded and attuned to spatial disparities [13].

1.5.2 Remote Sensing: Satellite-Based Insights for Poverty Assessment

Remote sensing introduces a transformative, high-resolution dimension to poverty mapping by providing granular spatial information across vast and often inaccessible regions. Through the analysis of satellite imagery, researchers can extract poverty-relevant indicators using visual proxies such as building materials, transportation networks, and infrastructure density. These visual cues uncover intricate spatial patterns related to settlement quality, resource accessibility, and infrastructural inequality—factors that are vital for understanding the geographic complexity and spatial distribution of poverty [14] [15] [16].

Remote sensing allows poverty mapping to move beyond traditional static indicators such as income or consumption, enabling the assessment of dynamic environmental and infrastructural factors that directly affect poverty levels. This aerial perspective provides valuable insights for identifying regions with infrastructural deficiencies, which often correspond to areas exhibiting higher levels of poverty.

Despite its advantages, remote sensing faces notable limitations. Issues such as restricted spatial resolution and the dependency on regularly updated datasets underscore the importance of integrating remote sensing with other complementary methods. A synergistic approach is essential to achieve a comprehensive and accurate understanding of poverty dynamics [17] [18].

1.5.3 Environmental and Spatial Dimensions of Poverty

In recent years, environmental stressors such as deteriorating air quality, water contamination, excessive noise, and exposure to hazardous waste have intensified beyond acceptable levels, posing significant challenges to human health and well-being [19]. A persistent concern in the field of environmental justice is the strong and unequal relationship between poverty and exposure to such environmental risks. A growing body of research suggests that economically disadvantaged populations are disproportionately affected by environmental hazards due to geographical, infrastructural, and structural inequities.

These communities often reside in areas with higher pollution levels, limited green space, poor sanitation, and reduced access to clean resources. This exacerbates their vulnerability to health risks and further deepens social and economic marginalization. The health impacts of environmental stressors ranging from respiratory and cardiovascular illnesses to developmental and psychological disorders can be especially severe among children and the elderly. For instance, exposure to pollutants like particulate matter, contaminated water, and industrial toxins has been linked to cognitive delays, weakened immune systems, and chronic conditions.

Such health burdens not only impair individual well-being but also result in higher medical expenses, reduced productivity, and limited educational attainment, particularly in resource-constrained settings. Consequently, environmental stressors can reinforce cycles of poverty and social exclusion, making it difficult for affected communities to break free from long-term deprivation. Understanding and addressing these interconnected challenges is essential for developing sustainable, inclusive, and health-equity-oriented policies.

1.5.4 Hybrid Approaches: Integrating Multi-Source Data for Holistic Poverty Analysis

Achieving a comprehensive understanding of poverty requires adopting a multifaceted perspective rather than relying on a single data source or analytical lens. Hybrid approaches to poverty mapping embody this principle by integrating diverse datasets and methodologies to develop a more realistic and context-sensitive representation of deprivation. For instance, satellite imagery and household survey data together provide insights into income levels and access to essential services, while remote sensing data captures geographical and environmental patterns. Government records offer additional information on social vulnerabilities, and mobile phone usage data reveals real-time behavioral and mobility trends. This integrated approach extends the analysis beyond the "what" of poverty to also encompass the "where" and "why," offering a deeper understanding of its spatial dimensions and underlying drivers [20] [21].

Further depth is achieved through triangulation techniques, which merge quantitative data with the richness of Participatory Poverty Assessments (PPAs) and social mapping. Quantitative survey findings are contextualized with community perspectives, bringing forward local experiences, challenges, and priorities. Participatory mapping workshops translate statistical data into spatial narratives, unveiling regional disparities and community-specific insights. This integrative process not only enhances the validity and relevance of findings but also ensures that proposed interventions are grounded in the lived realities of the affected populations.

The successful implementation of hybrid methods necessitates careful planning, technical expertise, and interdisciplinary collaboration, while maintaining strict adherence to ethical standards, particularly concerning data privacy and informed consent. Despite these challenges, the advantages are transformative: hybrid approaches enable a more profound understanding of poverty, facilitate targeted interventions, and promote empowerment of marginalized communities. Ultimately, they serve as a cornerstone for designing actionable, evidence-based strategies that foster inclusive and sustainable development [22].

1.6 Challenges in Existing Poverty Mapping Techniques

Despite progress in leveraging data and analytics for poverty estimation, several methodological and operational challenges persist in existing poverty mapping frameworks. These limitations undermine the reliability, timeliness, and applicability of poverty maps, particularly in developing regions where decision-making needs are urgent and context-sensitive. This section outlines three critical challenges that continue to hinder effective poverty mapping: data inconsistency and temporal lags, underutilization of geospatial and environmental features, and the interpretability gap in complex machine learning models.

1.6.1 Data Inconsistency and Temporal Gaps

One of the most pressing challenges in poverty mapping is the temporal and structural inconsistency of data sources. Traditional poverty assessments rely heavily on large-scale household surveys and national census data, which are typically collected at intervals of five to ten years. As a result, poverty estimates derived from such data quickly become outdated and fail to reflect current realities, especially in regions experiencing rapid socio-economic or environmental change.

Moreover, datasets often vary in spatial resolution, sampling methodology, and reporting standards, leading to inconsistencies across administrative boundaries and time periods. For instance, while some surveys provide data at the district level, others may only capture state-level aggregates, impeding fine-grained spatial analysis. These temporal gaps and mismatched scales limit the responsiveness of poverty mapping efforts, delaying critical interventions and compromising the relevance of policy decisions.

1.6.2 Under utilization of Geo spatial and Environmental Data

Although the potential of geospatial data in poverty analysis is increasingly recognized, its full integration into mainstream poverty mapping remains limited. High-resolution satellite imagery, nighttime light intensity, and environmental indicators such as the Air Quality Index (AQI) and radiance values offer crucial proxies for infrastructure quality, economic activity, and environmental risk exposure. However, these indicators are often overlooked or treated in isolation, rather than being systematically integrated with socioeconomic data.

Environmental stressors, in particular, are rarely incorporated into poverty modeling frameworks, despite their proven correlation with health outcomes, productivity loss, and long-term deprivation. For example, populations exposed to poor air quality often suffer from chronic health conditions that increase healthcare expenses and reduce income-generating potential factors directly linked to poverty. The lack of such contextual environmental variables results in incomplete models that fail to capture the multi-dimensional nature of poverty.

1.6.3 Model Interpretability and Local Relevance

With the growing adoption of machine learning and deep learning techniques in poverty prediction, another critical issue has emerged: the lack of model interpretability. Many state-of-the-art models deliver high predictive accuracy but provide limited transparency about how input features influence the final outcome. This lack of clarity undermines trust and usability, especially for policymakers who require clear explanations to justify targeted interventions.

Furthermore, models trained on generalized or national-level datasets often lack local relevance, ignoring region-specific socioeconomic dynamics, cultural factors, or environmental conditions. Without interpretability and contextual alignment, such models risk misclassifications or misguided targeting, thereby exacerbating rather than alleviating existing inequalities. Ensuring that models are not only accurate but also explainable and adaptable to local conditions is essential for translating predictive insights into actionable policy.

1.7 Motivation

Despite global progress in poverty reduction, recent setbacks caused by the COVID-19 pandemic, economic disruptions, and regional conflicts have significantly slowed progress. As of March 2024, approximately 8.9% of the world's population continues to live below the extreme poverty line of $2.15 (PPP) per day This persistent poverty, particularly in low- and middle-income countries, poses a major obstacle to achieving Sustainable Development Goal 1: No Poverty. As Kofi Annan aptly stated, "Without good data we're flying blind. If you can't see it, you can't solve it" [23]. His words emphasize a critical challenge when poverty remains underreported or invisible in data systems, it severely limits the effectiveness of targeted policy responses.

Traditional poverty assessment methods, which rely heavily on household surveys, suffer from infrequent data collection, high operational costs, and limited spatial resolution. These shortcomings make it difficult to capture the complex, multidimensional, and localized nature of deprivation. In response, there is an urgent need for innovative, technology-driven approaches that can overcome these data gaps. The integration of high-resolution satellite imagery, environmental indicators and advanced computational methods like artificial intelligence and machine learning provides a powerful framework for real-time, granular, and multidimensional poverty prediction. Such models can offer policymakers actionable insights, enabling more inclusive, evidence-based, and geographically targeted development strategies. India, with its vast population and cultural diversity, exemplifies the challenges of poverty alleviation in complex socio-economic settings. Despite notable economic growth, a large segment of the population remains poor and excluded from mainstream development. The poverty landscape in India reflects deep regional inequalities, with rural and urban areas facing unique sets of challenges. Madhya Pradesh, India's second-largest state by area and population, highlights this complexity. Although endowed with natural resources and cultural richness, the state continues to struggle with entrenched rural poverty, driven by low agricultural productivity, inadequate infrastructure, and limited access to essential services. Urban areas face their own challenges, including rapid population growth, overstretched infrastructure, and rising socio-economic disparities. These pressing issues underscore the necessity for data-driven and context-aware solutions to guide poverty alleviation efforts effectively in such diverse environments.

1.8 Research Scope

This research is designed to address the multidimensional and spatially dynamic nature of poverty by leveraging a combination of remote sensing, environmental indicators, and artificial intelligence techniques. The scope of the study is defined across three critical dimensions geographical, temporal, and technological each of which plays a key role in shaping the research design, data selection, modeling process, and applicability of results.

The geographical focus of this study is the Indian state of Madhya Pradesh, a region characterized by significant socio-economic diversity, widespread rural habitation, and high multidimensional poverty rates. Madhya Pradesh provides an ideal testing ground due to its varied topography, infrastructural gaps, and presence of both urban and remote rural settlements. This diversity allows for meaningful analysis of spatial poverty patterns across contrasting environments.

The state has also been selected for its data availability across multiple modalities, satellite imagery, air quality data, radiance measurements, and household survey responses making it a practical and relevant choice for conducting multimodal poverty prediction. By focusing on a subnational unit rather than the national scale, the study achieves higher granularity and policy relevance, enabling insights that can be applied to district- or block-level intervention planning.The study is temporally bounded by the years 2020 to 2023, during which all major datasets were acquired and synchronized for consistency.

1.8.1 Understanding the living conditions and infrastructural development as indicators of poverty

- **Objective:** To develop a predictive model that combines features extracted from daytime satellite imagery with household-level survey data for poverty classification using deep learning and machine learning techniques.
- **Rationale and Approach:** Traditional poverty assessments rely heavily on socioeconomic surveys, which offer valuable but limited insights when used in isolation. Meanwhile, daytime satellite imagery captures visual cues of built environment quality, infrastructure density, vegetation cover, and settlement structure factors that indirectly reflect economic conditions. By leveraging VGG16, a pretrained convolutional neural network, the aim is to automatically extract mean-

ingful spatial features from satellite images. The combined use of structured survey data and unstructured image data enables a multimodal learning approach, improving classification accuracy and interpretability.

- **Methodology:**
  - **Survey Data Collection:** A structured questionnaire consisting of 45 items was administered to households across selected districts of Madhya Pradesh, capturing indicators related to health, education, sanitation, employment, and housing.
  - **Satellite Image Acquisition:** High-resolution daytime satellite images were obtained for the same geographic coordinates from publicly available satellite data sources.
  - **Feature Extraction:** The VGG16 model is used to extract 4096-dimensional features from image tiles centred on surveyed households. Survey responses are aggregated and normalised to align with the spatial units of the imagery.
  - **Fusion and Classification:** A unified feature vector is constructed by concatenating the visual features extracted from imagery with the socioeconomic attributes derived from survey data. This multimodal feature set is then used to train machine learning classifiers, namely Random Forest, XGBoost, and Support Vector Machine (SVM) for predicting and classifying district-level poverty levels.
  - **Validation:** Accuracy metrics including Precision, Recall, F1-score, and ROC-AUC are used to evaluate performance. The

model's outputs are also mapped to assess spatial patterns

1.8.2 Understanding the Economic activities and environmental conditions as the indicators of poverty

- **Objective:** To incorporate environmental stressors specifically, Air Quality Index (AQI) and radiance data into a deep learning framework using nighttime satellite imagery to enhance the contextual accuracy of poverty predictions.

- **Rationale and Approach:** Environmental stressors play a critical but often overlooked role in poverty estimation. Poor air quality is linked to adverse health outcomes and economic vulnerability, while radiance (light intensity) at night correlates with infrastructure, electricity access, and economic activity. Nighttime light data from satellite sensors, combined with Air Quality Index (AQI) and radiance metrics, provide proxy indicators for developmental disparity. This module uses a modified SENet-154 architecture to jointly learn from both visual and contextual environmental inputs, offering a comprehensive view of poverty influenced by spatial and ecological conditions.

- **Methodology:**

  - **Data Acquisition:** Nighttime Light (NTL) images are obtained from the VIIRS (Visible Infrared Imaging Radiometer Suite) archiv AQI data is collected from Central Pollution Control Board (CPCB monitoring stations and interpolated to match spatial units. AQI and radiance features are input into the model's final layers to facilitate contextual learning.

- **Feature Extraction:** The SENet-154 model is fine-tuned to extract visual patterns from nighttime imagery. AQI and radiance features are fed into the final layers of the model to enable contextual learning.
- **Classification:** Fused features from SENet and environmental stressors are classified using ML algorithms (RF, XGBoost, SVM). Poverty classification is carried out at household or grid level.
- **Evaluation:** Classification results are assessed using standard performance metrics. Comparative analysis with the daytime model highlights the contribution of environmental data.

1.8.3 Spatial Autocorrelation and prediction of poverty clusters for targeted interventions

- **Objective:** To validate the spatial clustering and consistency of predicted poverty levels using spatial autocorrelation techniques
- **Rationale and Approach:** While classification metrics capture model performance statistically, they do not reveal the spatial structure of poverty. Spatial validation tools such as LISA and Moran's I provide insight into whether the predicted poverty patterns align with expected geographic clusters. This spatial layer of validation ensures that model outputs are not only accurate but also spatially coherent and policy-relevant.
- **Methodology:**
  - **Spatial Join and Mapping:** Predicted poverty levels are joined to spatial units (districts or grid cells) using GIS tools.

Global Moran's I Calculation: This metric is used to evaluate whether poverty values are spatially autocorrelated (i.e., clustered or dispersed).

LISA Cluster Mapping: Localized patterns are identified to detect hotspots (high-high) and cold spots (low-low) of poverty.

Interpretation: The clustering patterns are compared with known deprivation zones to evaluate model validity. Maps are produced to visualize the spatial distribution of poverty for policymakers.

1.9 Organization of the thesis

This thesis is organized into seven chapters, each contributing to the overall objective of developing a comprehensive and intelligent framework for multidimensional poverty prediction. The chapter-wise organization is as follows:

- **Chapter 1: Introduction to Poverty Prediction**

  This chapter provides a comprehensive introduction to the research problem, highlighting the importance of accurate and up-to-date poverty mapping in the context of Sustainable Development Goal 1 (No Poverty). It outlines the motivation, objectives, research gaps, and the key contributions of the study, along with a brief overview of the methodologies employed.

- **Chapter 2: Literature Review**

  This chapter reviews existing work in the areas of poverty estimation, remote sensing, environmental data integration, and machine learning techniques. It discusses traditional survey-based approaches as well as recent advancements using satellite imagery and artificial intelligence. The review identifies the limitations in current methods and establishes the research gap this thesis aims to address.

- **Chapter 3: Dataset Generation from Survey Data and Feature Engineering**

  This chapter details the methodology for data collection and processing. It explains the design of the household survey, the preprocessing and aggregation of responses, and the integration with district-level census data. The chapter also outlines the feature engineering strategies used to construct enriched input vectors for subsequent modelling tasks.

- **Chapter 4: Module 1 – Poverty Prediction Using Daytime Satellite Imagery and Survey Data**

  This chapter presents the first module of the study, where visual features are extracted from daytime satellite images using the VGG16 model. These features are combined with engineered survey-census data, and various machine learning classifiers are applied to predict poverty levels. The performance of each classifier is analyzed and evaluated.

- **Chapter 5: Module 2 – Nighttime Imagery with Environmental Indicators (AQI and Radiance)**

  This chapter describes the second module, which integrates features extracted from nighttime light images using the SENet-154 deep learning model, along with environmental indicators such as AQI and radiance. The combined feature set is used to train predictive models, with emphasis on understanding the spatial and environmental dimensions of poverty.

- **Chapter 6: Spatial Correlation and Poverty Prediction Index (PPI) Generation**

  This chapter focuses on spatial analysis using Local Moran's I and LISA to detect poverty clusters across regions. It also explains the methodology for computing the Poverty Prediction Index (PPI) by combining multidimensional features enhancing the interpretability and applicability of the results for policymakers.

- **Chapter 7: Conclusion and Future Scope**

  The final chapter summarizes the key findings and contributions of the research. It discusses the policy implications through the proposed framework and outlines the limitations of the study. Directions for future work, including model generalization and scalability to other regions.

- **References** This section compiles all the scholarly works, datasets, models, and frameworks cited throughout the thesis. It includes journal articles, government reports, survey instruments, and tools used for data processing, ensuring transparency and reproducibility of the research.

1.10 Graphical abstract of the overall thesis

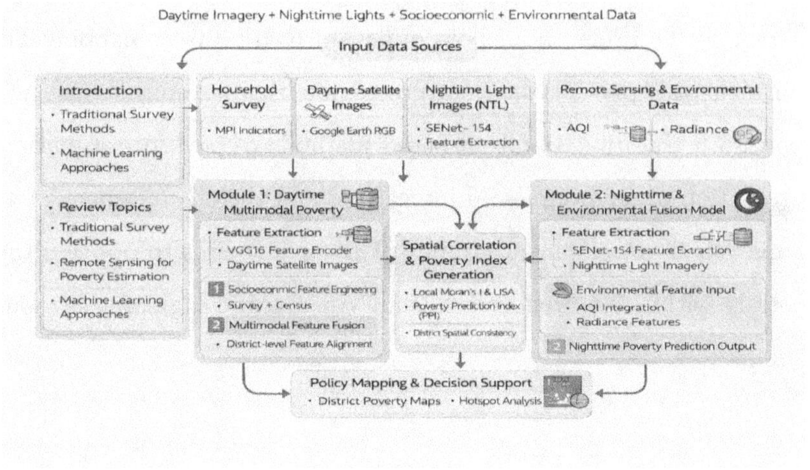

Figure 1.2: Graphical abstract of the Thesis

1.11 Summary

This chapter established the foundation for a comprehensive investigation into the integration of geospatial technologies, environmental stressors, and artificial intelligence for multidimensional poverty prediction. The research is motivated by the urgent need for high-resolution, real-time, and interpretable poverty maps that can inform targeted policy interventions aligned with Sustainable Development Goal 1 (SDG 1). The chapter began by framing poverty as a complex, multidimensional issue that cannot be fully captured by income measures alone. It introduced the rationale for combining traditional survey data with novel data sources such as daytime and nighttime satellite imagery, Air Quality Index (AQI), and radiance. The limitations of existing poverty mapping approaches such as temporal gaps, underutilization of environmental data, and the lack of model interpretability were critically examined. This chapter has clearly defined the objectives, rationale, and technological scope of the study, setting the stage for an in-depth analysis of data-driven poverty mapping.The following chapter presents a literature review that examines existing research on both traditional and AI-based methods of poverty estimation, the integration of environmental indicators, and the advancement of geospatial analysis in development studies. This review aims to position the current study within the broader academic context and highlight key gaps that it seeks to address.

Chapter 2

Literature Survey

Poverty is one of the most important challenges which is directly related to health, education, infrastructure, and environmental conditions. The traditional poverty assessment method using household surveys and census data is often time consuming, costly, and spatially limited, particularly in developing countries where up-to-date data are not available. To address these challenges, researchers have explored remote sensing technologies and machine learning (ML) algorithms as efficient tools to map, monitor, and predict poverty in diverse geographies. This chapter explores the evolving techniques for predicting poverty based on data, focusing particularly on the use of satellite imagery, multimodal data fusion, and Artificial Intelligence based predictive models. Furthermore, this survey includes studies that focus on multidimensional poverty indices (MPI), socioeconomic surveys, and environmental exposure data to predict not only income poverty, but also deprivations in health, education, and living standards. By critically reviewing recent literature, this survey seeks to highlight methodological trends, geographic applications, key findings, and research gaps, ultimately offering insights into how machine learning and remote sensing can support evidence-based poverty alleviation strategies in the era of

Sustainable Development Goals (SDGs).

2.1 Understanding Poverty: Definitions and Dimensions

Poverty is a complex and multidimensional phenomenon that extends beyond the mere absence of income or financial resources. It reflects the deprivation of fundamental capabilities necessary for a life of dignity encompassing access to adequate food, education, healthcare, shelter, clean water, and opportunities for social and economic inclusion [24]. Traditionally, poverty has been assessed through monetary thresholds, such as the international poverty line defined by the World Bank at $2.15 per day, which primarily captures extreme forms of income-based deprivation [25].

2.2 Poverty Measurement Techniques

2.2.1 Traditional and Multidimensional Poverty Measurement Approaches

This section reviews studies that utilize Multidimensional Poverty Index (MPI), census, and household survey data. The MPI [26], developed by the United Nations Development Programme (UNDP) in collaboration with the Oxford Poverty and Human Development Initiative (OPHI), offers a more comprehensive measure of poverty by encompassing indicators across health, education, and living standards. The MPI is based on the Alkire–Foster methodology, which employs a dual cutoff approach: first identifying deprivations within each dimension and then applying an overall poverty threshold determined by the weighted sum of these deprivations.

The Multidimensional Poverty Index (MPI) framework evaluates poverty across three core dimensions encompassing ten indicators: Health (child mortality, nutrition), Education (years of schooling, school attendance), and Living Standards (cooking fuel, sanitation, drinking water, electricity, housing, and assets). Each dimension contributes equally one-third to the overall index, with all indicators within a dimension receiving equal weight. A household is identified as multidimensionally poor when its total deprivation score reaches or exceeds 33.3% of the weighted indicators.

Large-scale census data can serve as a valuable resource for poverty mapping. In [27], the authors propose a semi-supervised deep learning framework that enhances poverty prediction by integrating limited household survey data with extensive but unlabeled census records. The approach employs a deep neural network to generate pseudo-labels for the census data, derived from patterns learned in the labeled survey samples. These pseudo-labeled records are subsequently used to retrain the model, thereby improving its generalization capability and spatial coverage in poverty estimation.

In [28] a detailed multidimensional poverty assessment focused on poor households in Guwahati, Assam, India was conducted using the Alkire–Foster methodology to construct a tailored MPI at the urban context . The study examines how factors such as migration status, occupational engagement, social identity, and literacy shape poverty alongside income.This work underscores the necessity of a comprehensive, context-sensitive approach to urban poverty measurement and suggests targeted interventions in education, employment, and living conditions to improve the well-being of vulnerable urban populations.

In [29] a comprehensive estimation of Multidimensional Poverty Index (MPI) across 82 natural regions in India, using 2011–12 data from the Indian Human Development Survey (IHDS) was conducted, which concluded that approximately 43% of India's population is multidimensionally poor, with an average poverty intensity of 45.5%, yielding an aggregate MPI of 0.193. They also show that the economic component accounts for about one-third of deprivations in most regions. This granular sub-national analysis emphasizes the heterogeneity of deprivation within states, highlighting the need for region-specific policy interventions and more nuanced welfare frameworks beyond income measures.

In summary, poverty is best understood and addressed through a comprehensive, multidimensional lens that considers income, capabilities, spatial, and environmental factors. This integrated approach provides policymakers with a more accurate roadmap for monitoring and improving welfare, and for designing effective anti-poverty strategies.

2.2.2 Remote Sensing Data as a Proxy for Economic Well-being

The study in [30] presents an approach that combines satellite imagery with machine learning to predict poverty. By employing a transfer learning framework, the authors first trained a convolutional neural network to predict nighttime light intensity from daytime satellite images, keeping lights as a proxy for economic activity. The learned features were then used to estimate asset-based poverty indicators from household survey data.

In [31], a deep learning framework was proposed that leverages publicly available satellite imagery to assess economic well-being across African countries. The study uses convolutional neural networks (CNNs) trained on high-resolution daytime satellite imagery, which capture visible indicators of infrastructure, agriculture, and development. These models are calibrated using household survey data to predict asset-based wealth indices at fine spatial scales. The authors demonstrate that their method can generate accurate, high-resolution poverty maps across diverse geographic regions, even in areas lacking recent or reliable data.

[32] explores the use of open-access satellite data and machine learning to map poverty in Belize, The authors utilize features derived from freely available satellite imagery such as vegetation, building density, and land use, combined with national census data to train predictive models for estimating poverty rates. In [33] authors proposed a multi-task deep learning framework to predict poverty from satellite imagery, the model is trained using convolutional neural networks (CNNs) on publicly available satellite images and validated against survey-based poverty indicators. In [33] a review was done on the growing role of satellite imagery in sustainable development goals (SDGs), emphasizing how remotely sensed data can provide timely, scalable, and cost-effective insights into critical global challenges such as poverty, agriculture, health, and environmental change.

In [34], authors present a novel approach for mapping human activity volumes using remote sensing imagery and deep learning techniques. The study develops a Deep Convolutional Neural Network (DCNN) model that integrates features from high-resolution satellite images to estimate the intensity of human activity in urban areas. By incorporating environmental features and the influence of neighboring regions termed as the neighbor effect, the model captures both localized and spatial contextual information.

The neighbor effect, representing the inherent nature of spatial autocorrelation in the volumes, is incorporated to improve the network. Convolutional Neural Network (CNN)-based approach for poverty estimation using satellite imagery was done in [35]. The study addressed a major challenge of spatial misalignment between coordinates of the region and the corresponding satellite imagery for which the poverty is to be estimated. This misalignment was shown to significantly reduce the predictive accuracy of CNN models. To address this issue, the authors proposed an ensemble modeling strategy incorporating grid-cell selection techniques, which effectively reduced the impact of coordinate errors.

In [36] [37], the researchers utilized the information provided by Night-time imagery on human activity through light intensity, while daytime images capture environmental and infrastructural details to demonstrate that the combination of both modalities significantly enhances predictive accuracy compared to using either one alone. The research highlights the potential of multimodal satellite data and deep feature integration for advancing socioeconomic mapping. In [38] authors proposed a method for poverty detection using satellite imagery combined with regression-based predictive modeling. The study focuses on estimating income levels in developing countries by analyzing satellite images, particularly focusing on features such as lighting intensity, infrastructure patterns, and land use. The authors develop a multitask learning model that incorporates both census data and satellite-derived features to improve accuracy in predicting economic indicators.

A case study in Guizhou, Southwest China was conducted [39] where the use of remote sensing and machine learning techniques to identify poverty-prone areas was done. They integrated high-resolution satellite imagery with geospatial and socioeconomic data to extract features such as land use, vegetation index (NDVI), and infrastructure density. These features are then used in various machine learning models, including decision trees and random forests to classify regions by poverty levels.

An efficient method for poverty mapping using high-resolution remote sensing imagery combined with deep learning was proposed in [40]. The study addresses the computational challenges of processing large-scale, high-resolution images by introducing a model that detects and counts semantically meaningful objects such as low-resolution buildings, roads, and vehicles. These object counts are then used as features in a regression model to predict village-level poverty in Uganda.

The fusion of NTL and geospatial features significantly enhances predictive performance compared to models using socioeconomic or NTL data alone. A comprehensive approach [41] was proposed for the evaluation of poverty at the county level by integrating machine learning, nightlight data (NTL) and a variety of geospatial indicators. Focusing on improving the spatial accuracy of poverty assessments, the study combines characteristics such as land cover, elevation, population density, and nighttime light intensity with poverty statistics using several machine learning algorithms, including Random Forest and XGBoost.

Transfer learning on satellite images plays a very important role. In [42], the authors explore the use of transfer learning in satellite imagery to predict socioeconomic indicators in municipalities in Brazil. By applying pre-trained convolutional neural networks (CNNs), the study extracts visual features from high-resolution images and applies them to estimate indicators such as income, education level, and housing quality. In [43] an investigation was carried out for the potential of nighttime light (NTL) data as a proxy for various social indicators relevant to the Sustainable Development Goals (SDGs). By analyzing satellite-derived NTL intensity in conjunction with global socioeconomic datasets, the study explores correlations between light emissions and indicators such as education, health, poverty, and access to basic services.

Study in [44] presents a comprehensive quantitative review of 60 studies that apply machine learning and satellite imagery for poverty prediction. Their analysis states how methodological factors, such as the type of welfare indicators they defined as asset-based "hard" vs. consumption-based "soft", and the choice of machine learning models, influence predictive performance.

To investigate the comparative effectiveness of convolutional neural networks (CNN) versus human expert-defined characteristics in the task of satellite poverty mapping, a study was conducted using Tanzanian data [45]. They stated that CNNs trained on medium-resolution satellite imagery consistently outperform models that rely on features designed by human experts. The CNN-based models were able to uncover complex spatial patterns and contextual visual cues such as settlement structure, vegetation, and road networks that human experts often overlook or underestimate.

Combining detailed ground-truth points with surrounding visual and spatial cues significantly improves the accuracy and robustness of fine-resolution poverty maps, offering a scalable solution for socio-economic monitoring in low-resource settings. In [46], a point-to-region co-learning framework for poverty mapping that effectively bridges the gap between precise point-level poverty annotations and broader regional contextual information was proposed. This dual-level architecture enables the model to capture both micro-level variation and macro-spatial patterns in socioeconomic conditions. Tested on high-resolution satellite imagery, the method demonstrates strong generalization capabilities, particularly in unlabeled or data-sparse regions.

In [47], a combination of multispectral VIIRS Nighttime Light data and satellite-derived features with machine learning models like Random Forest to detect and map poverty regions in Oran, Algeria was studied. Their case study states that integrating remote sensing indicators such as light intensity and land cover can reliably classify areas prone to poverty.

A review [48] focused on the role of transparency, interpretability, and domain expertise in the application of artificial intelligence to poverty mapping using satellite imagery was conducted. Analyzing 32 studies that utilize deep learning and remote sensing techniques, the authors emphasize the urgent need for explainable AI (XAI) models that not only yield accurate predictions but also provide meaningful insights that can be validated by domain experts.

Several other studies were referred to during the literature review that focus on the usage of Satellite Imagery. In [49], authors propose an ensemble learning model that uses CNN features extracted from satellite imagery to predict poverty levels, specifically nighttime light intensity as a proxy. The study in [50] leverages nighttime brightness data and satellite-derived features with neural networks to predict poverty rates at the state level in rural India. Their results demonstrate that satellite-based models outperform per capita GDP and traditional indicators, providing higher temporal resolution estimates. A semi-supervised multitask GAN framework trained on Landsat multispectral imagery [51] and DHS survey labels [52] was proposed in [53].

2.2.3 Semi-Supervised and Multimodal Learning Approaches

The study in [54] provides a geospatial analysis of multidimensional poverty patterns across rural and urban India, focusing on the spatial heterogeneity in poverty conditions. Using data from the National Family Health Survey (NFHS-5) and applying spatial contextualization techniques, the study identifies higher levels of multidimensional poverty in states such as Bihar, Jharkhand, Madhya Pradesh, and Uttar Pradesh, while Kerala, Sikkim, Goa, and Punjab exhibit relatively lower deprivation. In urban settings, Bihar and Uttar Pradesh show the highest urban poverty rates, whereas severe urban poverty is more prevalent in Himachal Pradesh, Uttarakhand, Odisha, West Bengal, and Punjab. Among all dimensions considered, nutrition emerges as the most significant contributor to both rural and urban poverty.

In [55], authors address the challenge of poverty prediction and mapping from various data sources, including mobile phone data, satellite imagery, and street maps. It proposes novel multi-view algorithms to address constraints and challenges, relax assumptions, and learn factorized representations. The study explores Gaussian process regression models [56] and Discriminative Factorized Subspace (DFS) [57] for representation learning. The research aims to generate spatially detailed poverty maps in a timely and cost-effective manner, aiding policymakers in making informed decisions.

In South Africa, [58] a study was conducted that leveraged remote sensing imagery and deep learning to analyze and predict poverty in South Africa, addressing the challenge of limited ground-level economic data in developing settings. They used pretrained CNN architectures, Inception V3 [59] and ResNet50 [60], that will estimate nighttime light intensity from daytime satellite images, and then used to predict district-level wealth index scores, cross-validated against Demographic and Health Survey (DHS) metrics.

Study in [61] explores the use of high-resolution satellite imagery and machine learning to identify urban poverty and assess housing inequality in Wuhan, China. The model showed the best performance, with an R^2 of around 0.53, indicating strong predictive accuracy. Spatial comparison using LISA [62] analysis revealed a close match between predicted and actual poverty clusters. The study highlights that simple, interpretable image features can effectively reflect socioeconomic disparities in urban environments and underscores the potential of remote sensing and ML as scalable tools for monitoring housing inequality and targeting development interventions.

A semi-supervised deep learning framework was proposed in [63] that enhances poverty prediction by utilizing limited survey-based poverty labels with unlabeled census data. Their approach employs a pseudo-labelling strategy, wherein a deep neural network (DNN) initially predicts poverty status for census units, which are then iteratively refined and used to train a more robust classifier. This method directly addresses the common challenge of label scarcity in household-level poverty datasets.

In [64], night-time light (NTL) data are recognized as a valuable proxy for assessing socioeconomic activity and sustainable development indicators. A significant milestone was the establishment of an open-access digital archive by the National Oceanic and Atmospheric Administration (NOAA) [65] and the National Geophysical Data Center (NGDC) [66] in 1992. This archive made available data from the Defense Meteorological Satellite Program's Operational Linescan System (DMSP/OLS) [67], which captured global night-time imagery daily over a span of more than two decades (1992–2013). The sensor operated at a spatial resolution of approximately 1–2.7 kilometers, covering earth swath as wide as 3000 km. The archived datasets were systematically processed into four main categories: daily and monthly time series, cloud-free composites, stable night-time light composites, and average visible light products. These data products have since been widely utilized for studying urbanization patterns, energy consumption, economic development, and poverty distribution especially in regions lacking timely and reliable socioeconomic statistics.

In [68], the launch of the Visible Infrared Imaging Radiometer Suite (VIIRS) aboard the Suomi NPP satellite in October 2011 marked a major leap in nighttime remote sensing. Equipped with the Day/Night Band (DNB), VIIRS offers substantial improvements over its predecessor DMSP/ OLS, including finer spatial resolution (742 m), radiometric calibration, and reduced light oversaturation or "blooming." These advancements have enhanced the precision of localized light source detection and positioned VIIRS/DNB as the standard for contemporary night-time light (NTL)-based monitoring. Building on this [69] presents a cost-efficient poverty mapping strategy for Uganda by combining transfer learning with reinforcement learning.

Instead of relying entirely on expensive high-resolution imagery, the model extracts features from low-resolution satellite data and uses reinforcement learning to dynamically select areas where high-resolution imagery is most needed. This adaptive sampling approach resulted in an 80% reduction in the number of high-resolution images required, significantly lowering costs while preserving prediction accuracy. Complementing this, [70] investigates the fusion of nighttime and daytime satellite imagery for poverty prediction using deep learning architectures such as VGGNet, InceptionNet, ResNet, and DenseNet. These features were further refined through LASSO regression, leading to improved predictive accuracy. Together, these studies highlight how innovations in sensor technology, data fusion, and learning strategies are transforming the efficiency, accuracy, and scalability of satellite-based poverty estimation.

2.2.4 Environmental Risk and Poverty Interlinkages

In recent years air quality index has increased above the expected levels. One of the main issues in the subject of environmental justice for a long time has been the connection between poverty and air quality. The idea that pollution affects poor communities is supported by a good amount of research that indicates these populations are more vulnerable to environmental risks, have less access to clean resources, and experience negative health effects.

Environmental pollution-related health differences have the potential to worsen already-existing socioeconomic inequities, entangling communities in cycles of ill health and poverty. Due to exposure to pollutants like lead and particulate matter, children in these locations may suffer from developmental problems and poorer academic performance, which may have an impact on their future economic prospects. Adults may experience higher medical expenses and decreased productivity as a result of illnesses linked to air pollution, further taxing their already low financial resources.

The study in [71] explores the link between socioeconomic status and environmental risk, highlighting how lower-income individuals are more exposed to hazards such as pollution, poor water quality, noise, overcrowding, substandard housing and unsafe work environments. These environmental risks negatively impact health and well-being, which impacts the socioeconomic health gradient. The study suggested that environmental justice is so important for health consequences mainly driven by exposure to various environmental factors, underscoring the need for research and policy interventions.

Recent research has begun to explore the intersection of environmental exposure and poverty, particularly the role of air pollution as both a driver and consequence of socioeconomic deprivation. The study in [72] presents a global-scale analysis that integrates high-resolution images with PM2.5$PM_{2.5}$ concentration data and harmonised household surveys in 211 countries. Their findings reveal that 94% of the global population lives in areas where ambient PM levels $_{2.5}$ exceed the WHO safety threshold. In particular, 716 million extremely poor people earning less than $1.90 per day are exposed to hazardous air quality, with a disproportionate burden borne by populations in Sub-Saharan Africa. The study also finds that lower-middle-income countries, driven by rapid industrialization, face particularly acute levels of exposure. These results highlight a profound challenge to environmental justice, where poverty and pollution converge to magnify health risks and constrain adaptive capacity. The authors emphasize the need for policies that decouple economic growth from environmental degradation, advocating inclusive access to clean-air technologies and healthcare equity.

In contrast, studies in [73] examine the poverty–pollution relationship in the United States, applying a machine learning framework to assess whether poverty levels correlate with environmental pollutant exposure at the county level. Utilizing a rich dataset of socioeconomic variables (poverty rates, unemployment) and pollution indices (PM., ozone, diesel particulates), the study employs feature engineering, LASSO regression, and model comparisons (AdaBoost, Elastic Net) across 37 curated variables. Surprisingly, the results indicate no significant correlation between poverty and pollutant levels across U.S. counties. Instead, exposure was found to correlate more strongly with localized factors such as industrial zoning policies and regulatory practices. These findings challenge the generalizability of environmental injustice narratives and point toward the need for geographically and contextually sensitive analyses when linking poverty and pollution exposure.

2.2.5 Machine Learning with Socioeconomic and Survey Data

An innovative framework was proposed in [74] to predict multidimensional poverty (MPI) at a street-block level in Medellín, Colombia, using open-source spatial data. Features extracted from OpenStreetMap (road networks, building footprints) and ESA land-cover datasets were combined, and several machine learning models, including Random Forest,

LightGBM, CatBoost, XGBoost, SVM, and linear regression, were used to estimate the MPI. The Random Forest model delivers the strongest results, achieving a mean absolute error (MAE) of 0.075 and generating spatial poverty estimates that closely align with the ground-truth distribution. The study demonstrates the feasibility of cost-effective, fine-grained poverty mapping without relying on expensive surveys, offering a scalable tool for policymakers to target poverty interventions at micro-urban scales.

To investigate poverty in Nigeria using a hybrid analytical approach that combines multidimensional poverty analysis with both traditional machine learning and deep learning techniques, a study was conducted [75]. The study begins with a Multiple Correspondence Analysis (MCA) of Nigeria Living Standards Survey data to construct a poverty index, followed by k-means clustering to label households as poor or non-poor. This labelled dataset is then used to train standard models, logistic regression, decision trees, and random forests on socioeconomic survey features. In a novel extension, they apply a Convolutional Neural Network (CNN) to high-resolution daytime satellite imagery (Google Maps) across Lagos and Jigawa states. Comparing approaches, they find that both survey-based ML and image-based CNN models capture poverty patterns, with each offering unique strengths. Their work demonstrates the feasibility of combining structured survey data and unstructured satellite imagery for scalable and interpretable poverty prediction, and suggests that a unified model leveraging both data sources could further enhance accuracy and policy relevance.

A feature-based deep neural framework for poverty prediction was proposed in [76] that leverages structured datasets using advanced deep learning and graph-based learning techniques. The model incorporates feature extraction, attention mechanisms, and graph learning to improve representation and contextual understanding of socioeconomic data. The framework is trained on census and geospatial attributes collected from urban and local government units, with supervised learning used to classify poverty levels. Unlike traditional statistical approaches, their architecture emphasizes data relationships and feature interactions, which are captured via a graph neural network (GNN) component. The use of an attention model further enhances the interpretability and focus of the learning process on the most relevant variables. The results show improved performance over baseline models, demonstrating the framework's utility for policymakers aiming to detect and target poverty more effectively in urban governance scenarios.

In [77] study focused on developing a machine learning–based framework to classify households into poverty and non-poverty groups using data from Jordan's Household Income and Expenditure Survey. The study applies and compares several supervised learning algorithms, including Random Forest, Logistic Regression, Decision Tree, Naïve Bayes, and K-Nearest Neighbours to identify the most effective model for poverty classification. Among the tested models, Random Forest performed best, achieving high accuracy and robustness in identifying vulnerable households. The research highlights key predictive features such as household size, education level, employment status, and geographic region. By providing a data-driven approach for rapid and cost-effective poverty classification, the study supports the development of targeted social welfare programs in Jordan and demonstrates the potential of ML methods in complementing traditional poverty measurement techniques.

An enhanced framework for poverty tracking and targeting in Jordan using feature selection techniques and machine learning algorithms to improve model accuracy and efficiency was proposed in [78]. The study utilizes household-level survey data and applies multiple supervised ML algorithms, including Random Forest, Gradient Boosting, and Logistic Regression to predict poverty status. A key contribution of this research is the use of feature selection methods to identify the most relevant socio-economic predictors, such as household size, income sources, regional location, and employment status. The Random Forest algorithm emerged as the most effective, yielding high accuracy and robustness in classifying poor households. This approach supports more targeted and equitable social policy design, aligning with the goals of Sustainable Development Goal 1 (No Poverty). The study also demonstrates how data-driven tools can enhance the decision-making process in public policy, particularly in low- and middle-income countries.

A machine learning-based poverty prediction model for Myanmar using a diverse set of open-source datasets, including nighttime light (NTL) intensity, OpenStreetMap features, and satellite-derived geospatial indicators, was proposed in [79]. The study aims to produce high-resolution poverty maps in data-scarce regions where conventional surveys are infrequent or unreliable. The authors employ Gradient Boosting Machines (GBM) and other supervised learning models trained on wealth index data from Demographic and Health Surveys (DHS) to estimate spatial poverty levels. The approach demonstrates that combining multi-source features such as infrastructure density, road networks, and light emissions yields higher predictive accuracy than using single-source data. The study not only reinforces the potential of low-cost, scalable, and repeatable poverty estimation strategies but also supports targeted policy-making and resource allocation for sustainable development in developing countries like Myanmar.

In [80], authors present a novel approach for estimating economic indicators such as GDP and total retail sales of consumer goods (TRSCG) using deep learning and remote sensing imagery. Specifically, the study leverages the ResNet50 deep residual neural network to extract features from satellite images classified by nighttime light intensity. These extracted features are then used in a ridge regression model to predict economic outcomes. The model achieved a high Pearson correlation coefficient of 0.85 for both GDP and TRSCG, outperforming traditional linear regression methods. The authors emphasize the accessibility and generalizability of their approach, as it uses publicly available satellite imagery, making it a low-cost and scalable method for estimating spatially explicit economic indicators. This framework demonstrates the effectiveness of combining deep feature extraction with statistical modelling in understanding regional economic conditions and provides a valuable tool for policymakers, especially in data-constrained settings.

Study in [81] explores the application of data mining techniques to predict household-level poverty in the Cuatro Santos region of Nicaragua, using data from a Health and Demographic Surveillance System (HDSS) [82]. The study applies several machine learning algorithms, including decision trees, random forests, and logistic regression, to a rich dataset containing over 50 variables spanning education, housing, employment, and health. The goal was to predict multidimensional poverty as defined by a locally adapted index. Among the models tested, random forests showed the highest predictive performance, with strong classification accuracy and variable importance insights. Key predictors of poverty included access to water, type of flooring, and household education levels. The authors emphasize that data mining can effectively complement traditional poverty measurement tools in resource-limited settings, offering locally adaptable, low-cost, and scalable solutions for identifying vulnerable households and informing targeted social interventions.

A comprehensive machine learning–based framework for poverty prediction, focusing on the integration of multidimensional indicators such as education, household size, employment, and housing quality, was developed in [83]. The study evaluates and compares several algorithms, including linear regression, neural networks, and boosting methods (e.g., XGBoost), to identify which model performs best in predicting poverty status based on socio-economic survey data. Neural networks and boosting algorithms demonstrated superior accuracy and generalizability compared to traditional regression models. The study emphasizes the flexibility and scalability of machine learning in processing complex, high-dimensional poverty data, enabling more accurate and real-time poverty assessments. The author concludes that leveraging such models can support evidence-based policymaking, particularly in developing economies where traditional poverty assessments are expensive or infrequent.

2.3 Research Gaps

Over the past decade, significant strides have been made in poverty prediction and mapping through the use of satellite imagery, machine learning, and big data analytics. These advancements have enabled researchers and policymakers to move beyond traditional survey-based methods and explore scalable, data-driven solutions for identifying and addressing poverty. Despite these efforts, many challenges remain. Existing approaches often fall short in capturing the multidimensional and spatially dynamic nature of poverty, particularly in low-resource and data-scarce regions. The following research gaps highlight the critical areas that require further investigation to build more accurate, inclusive, and actionable poverty prediction models:

1. **Limited Effectiveness of Nighttime Light Data in Isolation:** Nighttime light (NTL) data is helpful in showing areas of economic activity, but using it alone for poverty mapping has limitations, especially in rural areas where there is a lack of artificial light. These regions may still have important economic or social activities that NTL fails to detect due to a lack of artificial lighting. As a result, poverty in rural areas is often underestimated, while urban areas may be overrepresented.

2. **Lack of Multimodal Data Integration:** Current models often fail to incorporate complementary data sources such as high-resolution daytime satellite imagery, infrastructure maps, socioeconomic surveys, and night-time imagery. The absence of such multimodal integration restricts the ability to capture factors like agricultural productivity,

road accessibility, and housing quality essential for accurate poverty estimation.

3. **Lack of inclusion of Environmental deprivation indicators:** In countries like India, where living conditions are affected by environmental factors, weather conditions, deforestation, etc, a significant gap exists in integrating environmental stressors such as air pollution, radiation and land degradation, etc, into poverty prediction frameworks. These conditions are closely linked with poor health, livelihood conditions.

4. **Limited Insight into Ground-Level Realities:** Remote sensing alone cannot capture qualitative aspects of poverty, such as access to healthcare, education, or social marginalization. The lack of integration of participatory and qualitative data, like household-level surveys, limits the multidimensional understanding of poverty dynamics.

2.4 Problem Statement

Existing techniques in Poverty prediction often rely on individual data sources such as household surveys or satellite imagery and thus fail to capture the multidimensional, spatial, and environmental complexities of poverty. Current methodologies do not effectively integrate socio-economic, environmental, spatial, and economic indicators, nor do they use computer vision-based AI techniques to detect localized patterns of Poverty. As a result, many poverty maps remain outdated, low in resolution, and insufficiently actionable for timely policy interventions. Therefore, it is proposed to integrate diverse data sources, including survey responses, daytime and nighttime satellite imagery, air quality (AQI), and radiance data, to construct a multimodal deep learning-based poverty prediction model. The research aims to generate fine-grained, up-to-date poverty maps that more accurately reflect on-the-ground realities and support evidence-based policymaking. The goal is to support smarter and more targeted policy decisions to reduce poverty, in line with Sustainable Development Goal 1.

2.5 Objectives

- To identify the most relevant features from textual data, including household-level survey data and district-level census information that correlate with poverty.
- To apply feature engineering to both text and image data for multimodal analysis.
- To design a deep learning-based integrated framework for poverty prediction, focusing on the Madhya Pradesh region of India. The framework combines socioeconomic features from text data with visual features extracted from daytime satellite imagery using convolutional neural networks.
- To develop a hybrid deep learning–machine learning framework using nighttime light imagery and environmental variables to improve poverty classification accuracy and validate spatial coherence of predicted clusters in Madhya Pradesh.

2.6 Summary and Discussion

This chapter provided a comprehensive review of the evolving methodologies and data sources used in poverty prediction, with a focus on the integration of geospatial technologies, environmental indicators, and artificial intelligence. The review began by examining traditional poverty estimation techniques, including survey and census-based methods, highlighting their value in capturing socioeconomic indicators while also noting their limitations in terms of spatial resolution, temporal frequency, and adaptability to dynamic conditions.

Subsequently, the chapter explored advancements in remote sensing and the use of satellite imagery, both daytime and nighttime for deriving poverty proxies such as housing quality, infrastructure, and light intensity. Studies using deep learning models like CNNs and transfer learning approaches were discussed, emphasizing their potential to extract latent features that correlate with economic deprivation.

The role of environmental stressors such as air pollution (AQI), radiance, and climatic conditions was also examined. These factors, though often overlooked in poverty modeling, were shown to be crucial contributors to health and economic vulnerabilities. Literature supporting the use of AQI and radiance as indirect indicators of deprivation justified their inclusion in this study's framework.

Additionally, the review highlighted the growing adoption of multimodal and hybrid approaches where survey data, imagery, and environmental variables are fused to improve prediction accuracy and contextual relevance. Limitations in current models, particularly regarding interpretability, local relevance, and the lack of spatial validation, were critically analyzed. Techniques such as LISA and Moran's I were identified as essential tools for validating the spatial integrity of poverty estimates.

Overall, this chapter has established the conceptual and empirical foundation for the proposed research. It identifies critical gaps such as the underutilization of environmental stressors, limited multimodal integration, and inadequate spatial validation that this thesis aims to address. These insights will inform the methodological design presented in the following chapter, where the proposed dual-module geospatial AI framework is detailed.

Chapter 3

Dataset Generation from Survey Data and Feature Engineering

To gain a micro-level understanding of poverty and residents' daily living conditions, we administered a household-level survey. This chapter outlines the process of generating a household survey dataset. The survey contains 45 questions that focus on key dimensions of poverty, including housing quality, access to basic services, educational attainment, health conditions, and technological integration. Each response was linked to a specific district for analysis of economic and developmental conditions.

The purpose of conducting this primary survey was to create a data set that provides more detailed ground-level information on household well-being. National census data provides important district-level information, but it often does not consider differences and details about how each household lives its daily life. This survey is a very important tool for understanding inequalities within the district and identifying poverty-related indicators that may not be fully represented in official statistics.

This dataset provides us with a base for multidimensional poverty analysis by finding correlations between household-level poverty and broader socio-economic factors.

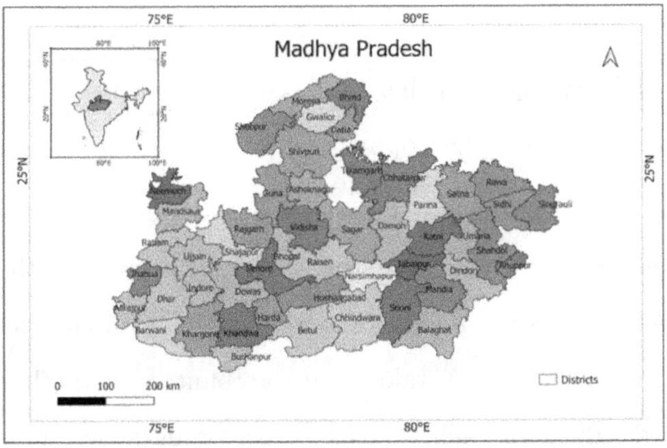

Figure 3.1: Administrative map of Madhya Pradesh, India.

3.1 Survey Coverage and Design

Our study focuses on the Madhya Pradesh region of India, as shown in Figure 3.1. ,We conducted a detailed survey across all 50 districts of Madhya Pradesh. Madhya Pradesh had a poverty rate of around 31.6% according to the World Bank's estimates in 2020. This means that nearly one-third of the population in the state lives below the poverty line [84].

The questions were framed to align with the indicators used in the Multidimensional Poverty Index (MPI). The questionnaire focused on the following areas:

1. Housing and Infrastructure: Type of dwelling, number of rooms, electricity, and water source.
2. Education: Years of schooling, highest qualification, distance to school.
3. Health: General health status, chronic illness, access to medical facilities.
4. Economic Activity: Sources of income, employment, and cooking fuel

used.

5. Social and Digital Inclusion: Access to markets, technology, migration, and community development.

For this purpose, we framed a questionnaire of 45 questions. The questionnaire was floated in the form of a survey in the 50 districts of the Madhya Pradesh region. The responses captured a wide range of values across the districts, taking into account both the highest and lowest observed values for each variable. These ranges were later considered for normalization, ensuring comparability across districts when merging with census data. Ethical standards were taken into account during data collection. We obtained consent from participants, explaining the research's purpose and their involvement. Consent was collected in a way that suited local preferences. The personal information column was anonymized and the data was stored securely with limited access. The data collected was used only for research, adhering to data protection regulations. All data is stored securely and only accessed by authorized personnel.

Table 3.1 given below, provides details of the multidimensional poverty index Questionnaire for Madhya Pradesh.

3.2 Process and Workflow

Questionnaire was floated in the different districts of Madhya Pradesh region through various resources in the form of Google Form as shown in Figure 3.2.

Table 3.1: Survey Questions based on Poverty Indicators

Q No	Question	Low Range	High Range
1	How many people are in your household?	1	10
2	What is the highest educational achievement reached by anyone in your household?	5	12
3	How many years of schooling have the adults in your household completed?	0	12
4	What is the distance to the nearest school from your residence?	1	30
5	On a scale of 1 to 5, how would you assess the overall health status of your household members?	1	5
6	Have any members of your household experienced chronic illnesses in the past year?	No	Yes
7	Does your household have access to electricity?	No	Yes
8	Your household primarily gets its drinking water from?	Natural	Tap Water
9	Describe the housing conditions by indicating the number of rooms available	1	6
10	How does your household primarily fuel its cooking activities?	Natural /LPG	Traditional Fuel
11	On a scale from 1 to 5, how would you assess the condition of roads in your neighborhood?	1	5
12	Does public transportation serve your area?	No	Yes
13	On a scale from 1 to 5, how would you rate the status of basic telecommunications services?	1	5
14	On a scale of 1 to 5, how would you rate the status of internet services?	1	5
15	Does your area typically have consistent access to electricity?	No	Yes
16	What are the primary sources of income for your household?	Agricultural	Non-Agricultural / Service
17	What is the primary type of housing material used in your households??	Kutcha	Pucca
18	On a scale from 1 to 5, how would you evaluate the productivity and profitability of agricultural activities in your vicinity?	1	5
19	What limitations or challenges are faced in agricultural practices in your area?	No	Yes
20	Do you have knowledge of any government welfare programs in place?	No	Yes
21	Have you utilized any government welfare schemes?	No	Yes
22	On a scale from 1 to 5, how do you perceive the level of poverty in your community?	1	5
23	Are educational facilities readily accessible within your community?	No	Yes
24	On a scale from 1 to 5, how would you rate the quality of education in local schools?	1	5

Q No	Question	Low Range	High Range
25	Are healthcare services easily accessible and affordable in your area?	No	Yes
26	On a scale from 1 to 5, how would you rate the nutritional status of children in your household?	1	5
27	Are you experiencing difficulties in accessing sufficient and nutritious food?	No	Yes
28	Are there any challenges you encounter in securing stable employment?	No	Yes
29	Are there any environmental challenges your community face?	No	Yes
30	On a scale from 1 to 5, how does the environment affect your daily life and livelihood?	1	5
31	Did you receive any government assistance within the past year?	No	Yes
32	On a scale from 1 to 5, how effective do you find government support programs?	1	5
33	Are financial services readily available in your area, such as banking facilities?	No	Yes
34	On a scale from 1 to 5, how challenging has it been for you to access financial services?	1	5
35	On a scale from 1 to 5, how prepared is your community for natural disasters like floods, droughts, etc.?	1	5
36	On a scale from 1 to 5, how accessible are markets and shopping facilities in your locality?	1	5
37	On a scale from 1 to 5, how challenging is it for you to access basic amenities?	1	5
38	Are there any community-led initiatives for development in your area?	No	Yes
39	On a scale from 1 to 5, how actively do community members participate in local development efforts?	1	5
40	Has there been any migration from your community?	No	Yes
41	On a scale from 1 to 5, how would you rate your access to modern technology and information?	1	5
42	On a scale from 1 to 5, how has the adoption of technology influenced your livelihood and standard of living?	1	5
43	On a scale from 1 to 5, how safe do community members feel in their neighborhood?	1	5
44	On a scale from 1 to 5, how effective are partnerships between the community and external organizations?	1	5
45	On a scale from 1 to 5, how do you envision the future of your community regarding poverty alleviation?	1	5

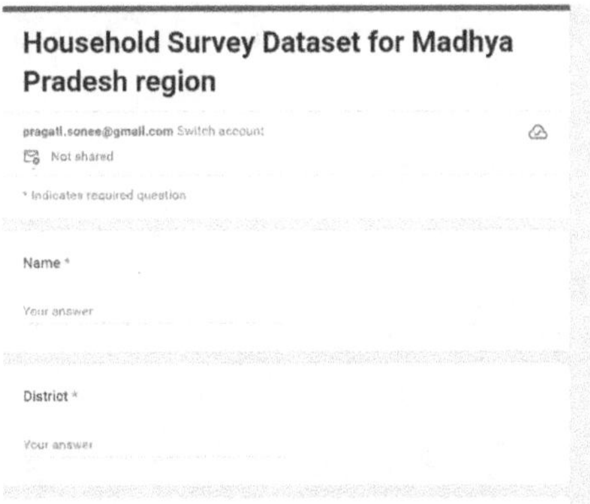

Household Survey Dataset for Madhya Pradesh region

pragati.sonee@gmail.com Switch account

Not shared

* Indicates required question

Name *

Your answer

District *

Your answer

Figure 3.2: Google Form for taking responses

It may be noted that certain survey variables were collected using threshold-based response options to align with the deprivation logic of the Multidimensional Poverty Index (MPI). Although this limits fine-grained variability, the design is appropriate for district-level poverty classification, where the presence or absence of deprivation is more informative than marginal differences

3.3 Processing of the Survey Responses

To improve the reliability and robustness of poverty prediction, household-level primary survey data were systematically aggregated to the district level for analysis. Figure 3.3 presents the raw responses collected from the survey.

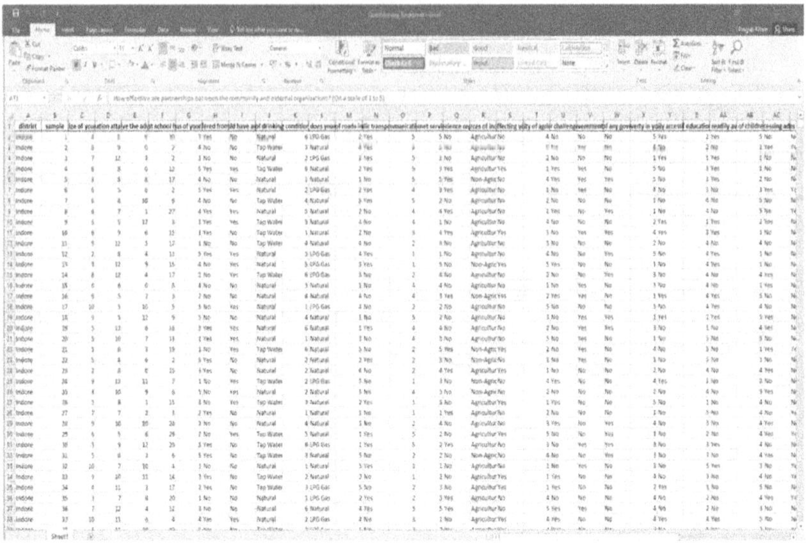

Figure 3.3: Responses Collected from the Survey

3.3.1 Survey Data Aggregation

The responses from the structured survey were collected at the household level. To enable proper analysis, the responses were aggregated at the district level using the following normalization strategy:

Table 3.2: Question Types and Pre-processing Strategies

Type	**Questions**	**Strategy**
Numerical (continuous/discrete)	Q1, Q2, Q3, Q4, Q9	Normalize to 0–1 scale using min-max normalization
Likert Scale (1–5)	Q5, Q11, Q13, Q14, Q18, Q22, Q24, Q26, Q30, Q32, Q34–37, Q39, Q41–45	Normalize to 0–1 by dividing response by 5
Binary (Yes/No)	Q6–8, Q10, Q12, Q15, Q17, Q19–21, Q23, Q25, Q27–29, Q31, Q33, Q38, Q40	Encode as 0 = No, 1 = Yes
Nominal/Categorical (Non-binary)	Q8, Q10, Q16	Map to ordinal scale if possible; else apply one-hot encoding [85] or create poverty-risk proxy scores

Numeric responses (number of schooling years, household size, access ratings on a 1–5 scale) were averaged using mean aggregation.

3.3.1.1 Mean Aggregation for Numeric Survey Responses

Let:

- x_{ij} be the response to question j from household i in district d,
- n_d be the number of surveyed households in district d,

Then the aggregated district-level value for question j is calculated as Equation 3.1 given below:

$$\bar{x}_j^d = \frac{1}{n_d} \sum_{i=1}^{n_d} x_{ij} \tag{3.1}$$

This formula is applied to variables such as household size, years of schooling, distance to school, and other 1–5 scale ratings.

3.4 Data Cleaning

Raw survey data often contain errors, inconsistencies, and missing values, which must be addressed through systematic data cleaning and preprocessing to ensure accuracy and reliability in subsequent analysis. Before using the collected responses for poverty prediction, it was essential to refine the dataset through a systematic cleaning process. Data cleaning ensures that duplicate entries are removed, incomplete or invalid responses are appropriately handled, and categorical variables are standardized for compatibility with statistical and machine learning models. Furthermore, given the spatial nature of this study, geolocation validation was performed to confirm the accuracy of GPS-tagged responses and to enable reliable integration with census and satellite imagery. This step produced a high-quality, consistent, and reliable dataset that served as the foundation for subsequent encoding, transformation, and predictive modeling. Data Cleaning is performed as explained in the sub-section 3.4.1

3.4.1 Removal of Duplicate entries

The first step involves identifying and removing duplicate survey records that may have been introduced during data entry or multiple submissions. Duplicate entries can bias statistical analysis and lead to inflated sample sizes, reducing the reliability of results. A unique identifier, such as a household ID or GPS coordinate, was used to detect repeated responses.

Only one valid record was retained, ensuring that the dataset contained unique, representative households.

3.4.2 Handling Missing Values

Raw survey data often contains incomplete responses. During data inspection, missing values were observed primarily in the following attributes: household income category, housing material, sanitation facility, cooking fuel, and access to healthcare services. These missing entries were predominantly due to incomplete survey responses.

The initial dataset comprised 18,120 household records. After handling missing values through imputation and the removal of records with excessive missingness, 17,640 records were retained for analysis, corresponding to a data retention rate of 97.3%.

Table 3.3: Summary of Rows Dropped per Attribute Due to Missing Values

Attribute	**Rows Dropped**	**Reason**
Income Category	59	Dropped due to missing values
Housing Material	23	Dropped due to missing values
Sanitation Facility	189	Dropped due to missing values
Cooking Fuel	23	Dropped due to missing values
Healthcare Access	186	Dropped due to missing values
Total	**480**	Total rows dropped across all attributes

This step systematically addressed missing values to prevent data loss or model bias:

- Identify Missing Values: Missing entries in both numeric and categorical fields were detected.
- Imputation: Missing numeric data was replaced with central tendency measures (mean or median), and categorical values were imputed using the mode (most frequent response).

- Row Dropping: If a record contained an excessive number of missing values, it was discarded to avoid distortion.
- Extreme/Invalid Values: Outliers and logically inconsistent responses (e.g., negative income, unrealistic age) were flagged and corrected or removed.

This ensured that the dataset remained complete, consistent, and free from extreme distortions.

3.4.3 Categorical Normalization and Aggregation

To prepare the predominantly textual and categorical survey data for machine learning, we implemented a harmonization and aggregation pipeline. This ensured that all features were represented in a consistent numerical format suitable for analysis and modeling.

1. Normalization and Encoding of Household-Level Data

- **Text Normalization.** Inconsistent free-text entries (e.g., "High school "HS," "12th pass") were mapped to a controlled set of standardized categories using rule-based matching.
- **Numerical Encoding.** Numerical encoding was applied to convert categorical variables into machine-readable formats based on their intrinsic characteristics. The resulting categorical variables were transformed as follows:
  - **Nominal features:** Nominal variables, which do not possess any inherent order, were encoded using one-hot encoding. The nominal categories considered were:

    * **Occupation Type:** Agricultural, Non-Agricultural/Service
    * **Housing Material:** Kutcha, Pucca
  - **Ordinal features:** Ordinal variables were encoded using label (ordinal) encoding to preserve their inherent ordering. In the case of education level, the variable was initially recorded as an ordinal attribute with response values ranging from 0 to 12 years of schooling, representing increasing levels of educational attainment. During preprocessing, this variable was subsequently used in a deprivation-oriented manner to distinguish households based on basic schooling completion, while retaining the ordinal nature of the original responses. This approach maintains consistency with the questionnaire design and aligns with the objectives of poverty classification.

- **Dataset Harmonization.** To enable merging with external sources (e.g., census data), category labels and coding schemes were aligned across datasets to ensure compatibility.

This stage transforms raw, unstructured categorical responses into a structured numerical matrix at the household level.

2. District-Level Aggregation

Following encoding, household-level data were aggregated to the district level to obtain a concise profile for each region.

Binary Variables. For binary responses (e.g., access to electricity: Yes/No), values were cast to numeric (Yes=1, No=0) and aggregated as proportions.

Proportion Calculation. The proportion of households in district d affirming condition j is as Eq 3.2 below :

$$p_{d,j} = \frac{1}{n_d} \sum_{i=1}^{n_d} I\left(x_{i,j} = 1\right), \tag{3.2}$$

where $x_{i,j}$ is a binary indicator variable that takes the value 1 if household i satisfies condition j, and 0 otherwise. The indicator function $I(\cdot)$ returns 1 when the condition is true and 0 when it is false.

This aggregation was applied to all relevant binary indicators, including access to electricity, water source, and modern cooking fuel. The pipeline yields a compact dataset in which each row represents a district characterized by aggregated socio-economic indicators derived from the original household-level survey.

3.4.4 Geolocation Validation

To enable integration with spatial and satellite data, ensuring geolocation accuracy and respondent privacy was critical. The following validation steps were performed:

- Anonymization: Personally identifiable information (names, addresses) was removed to protect respondent privacy.
- Records Without Location: Any entries lacking valid location information were dropped if they could not be matched with imagery or census polygons.
- GPS Validation: Geotagged survey responses were checked for valid latitude/longitude ranges and corrected if necessary.
- Final Review: A consistency check was carried out to confirm the

integrity of the dataset. In the final review stage, multiple consistency checks were performed to ensure the internal validity and integrity of the dataset. These included:

1. Logical consistency checks, such as verifying coherence between education level and occupation type, household size and number of rooms, and access to electricity versus reported lighting sources.
2. Cross-variable validation, ensuring alignment between related attributes (e.g., cooking fuel type and kitchen availability, housing material and sanitation access).
3. Geospatial consistency checks, confirming that household locations fell within valid district boundaries and matched corresponding census polygons.
4. Duplicate record verification, where repeated or near-identical responses were identified and removed.

These checks ensured that the retained records were logically consistent, spatially valid, and suitable for integration with satellite imagery and census-based datasets

This step guaranteed that only spatially accurate and anonymized records were retained, enabling safe integration with geospatial datasets such as satellite imagery and census maps.

Upon completion of these preprocessing stages, the resultant dataset was cleaned, anonymized, and geospatially validated. Systematic handling of duplicates and missing values, coupled with the normalization of categorical variables and spatial checks, ensured its integrity. This prepared the data for robust integration with census and satellite datasets, facilitating subsequent analysis and poverty prediction.A stepwise view of record retention is provided in Table 3.4.

Table 3.4: Summary of Data Cleaning Process

Cleaning Step	Before Cleaning	After Cleaning	Retained (%
Initial Dataset	18,378	18,378	100.0%
Duplicate Removal	18,378	18,120	98.6%
Handling Missing Values	18,120	17,640	97.3%
Outlier/Invalid Value Treatment	17,640	17,410	98.7%
Categorical Normalization	17,410	17,410	100.0%
Geolocation Validation	17,410	16,980	97.5%
Final Cleaned Dataset	18,378	16,980	**92.4%**

3.5 Label Assignment

For supervised poverty prediction, a labeled dataset is essential. We created this by defining a binary classification task, categorizing each household or district as "poor" or "non-poor." Labels were assigned using a combination of the Multidimensional Poverty Index (MPI) and local Below Poverty Line (BPL) values, ensuring the ground truth was both internationally benchmarked and relevant to Madhya Pradesh. This critical step transformed the raw data into a format ready for predictive modeling.

3.5.1 Defining Poverty

The first step involved establishing a clear definition of poverty. Poverty was not viewed solely in terms of income, but as a multidimensional construct, covering education, health, and standard of living indicators. Threshold criteria were derived from district-level MPI scores and official BPL statistics, both of which are widely used measures for identifying deprived households. This dual basis ensured that the labels reflected both household-level deprivation and regional poverty prevalence.

3.5.2 Threshold Criteria

The derived threshold values for categorizing poor and non-poor as per MPI(Multi-Dimensional Poverty Index) and BPL (Below Poverty Line) are as follows:

If MPI ≥ 0.2, then the household is categorized as poor.

MPI $< 0.2 \rightarrow$ Household categorized as Non-Poor

Additionally, if the percentage of Below Poverty Line households [86] in a district was 50% or more, then all households in that district were assigned the Poor label.

This dual thresholding helped account for cases where household MPI scores were borderline, but the district as a whole suffered from widespread poverty.

3.5.3 Assign Poverty Labels per District

Labels were then assigned at the district level. Every household in a district received the same classification once the thresholding rules were applied. This approach avoided inconsistencies within districts and ensured that the classification aligned with regional socio-economic realities.

3.5.4 Integration with Final Dataset

Finally, the assigned labels were integrated into the structured dataset as a new column called poverty_label. This transformed the dataset from an unlabeled survey collection into a supervised learning dataset. The resulting dataset now contained both predictor features (socio-economic and census indicators) and the dependent variable (poverty_label), which was essential for training and validating the machine learning models.

3.5.5 District-wise Distribution of Poor and Non-Poor Households (Pre-Labeling)

Although the final classification assigns a single poverty label to each district, the percentages reported in Table 3.5 , Table 3.6 and Table 3.7 represent pre-labeling household poverty proportions and are provided to ensure transparency of the district-level labeling process.

Table 3.5: District-wise Percentage of Poor and Non-Poor Population (Pre-Labeling)

District	Poor (%)	Non-Poor (%)
Alirajpur	78.67	21.33
Anuppur	34.84	65.16
Ashoknagar	41.94	58.06
Balaghat	29.13	70.87
Barwani	71.62	28.38
Betul	33.52	66.48
Bhind	26.45	73.55
Bhopal	51.96	48.04
Burhanpur	44.08	55.92
Chhatarpur	39.87	60.13
Chhindwara	28.63	71.37
Damoh	45.09	54.91
Datia	31.14	68.86
Dewas	22.45	77.55

Table 3.6: District-wise Percentage of Poor and Non-Poor Population (Pre-Labeling)

District	Poor (%)	Non-Poor (%)
Dhar	58.24	41.76
Dindori	64.71	35.29
Guna	37.66	62.34
Gwalior	19.84	80.16
Harda	27.12	72.88
Hoshangabad	23.41	76.59
Indore	16.88	83.12
Jabalpur	20.97	79.03
Jhabua	74.83	25.17
Katni	32.18	67.82

Table 3.7: District-wise Percentage of Poor and Non-Poor Population (Pre-Labeling)

District	Poor (%)	Non-Poor (%)
Khandwa	41.25	58.75
Khargone	55.74	44.26
Mandla	59.88	40.12
Mandsaur	21.94	78.06
Morena	28.76	71.24
Narsinghpur	24.18	75.82
Neemuch	19.33	80.67
Panna	48.55	51.45
Raisen	61.62	38.38
Rajgarh	15.61	84.39
Ratlam	34.77	65.23
Rewa	43.92	56.08
Sagar	36.44	63.56
Satna	38.81	61.19
Sehore	47.35	52.65
Seoni	31.69	68.31
Shahdol	46.27	53.73
Shajapur	18.94	81.06
Sheopur	52.88	47.12
Shivpuri	35.41	64.59
Sidhi	49.16	50.84
Singrauli	44.73	55.27
Tikamgarh	40.59	59.41
Ujjain	17.82	82.18
Umaria	46.91	53.09
Vidisha	50.66	49.34

3.6 Summary

This chapter detailed the process of dataset generation through a comprehensive field survey conducted across all 50 districts of Madhya Pradesh. The study aimed to capture multidimensional socio-economic indicators aligned with the Multidimensional Poverty Index (MPI) framework, covering dimensions such as health, education, and living standards. Data collection was carried out using both paper-based forms and mobile applications to ensure accuracy and accessibility, even in remote regions.

The survey design incorporated structured questions on household demographics, access to essential services, infrastructure quality, and income sources, ensuring compatibility with secondary datasets such as census information, AQI, and radiance data. Special attention was given to sampling strategies to maintain representativeness and reduce bias.

Post-collection, the survey data underwent rigorous preprocessing steps, including data cleaning, handling missing values, and standardizing variables for integration with other geospatial and environmental datasets. The final processed dataset served as a critical input for both the daytime satellite imagery-based model and the nighttime light and environmental variable-based model, enabling robust multimodal poverty prediction.

By establishing a reliable and context-specific ground truth dataset, this chapter laid the foundation for model training, validation, and spatial analysis in subsequent chapters.

Chapter 4

Poverty Prediction Using Daytime Satellite Imagery and Survey Data

The present chapter represents the first module of this research, focusing on the integration of household survey data with daytime satellite imagery for predicting poverty. The introductory chapter established the broader motivation of leveraging multimodal geospatial and socioeconomic data to advance the monitoring of Sustainable Development Goal 1 (SDG 1), and. This chapter narrows the scope to examine how visible indicators of development, when combined with traditional socioeconomic characteristics, can improve the precision of poverty estimation. By focusing on daytime imagery, this chapter explores the capacity of high-resolution satellite data to capture physical and infrastructural characteristics together with cleaned and standardized household survey and census data. These features form the basis for developing and validating machine learning models aimed at classifying poverty outcomes.

4.1 Introduction

The methods for poverty prediction discussed in the literature rely on the image and textual data individually for poverty assessment. They fail to consider critical factors. On one hand, image methods does not cover socioeconomic factors such as income, education, and health. Images can only capture visible features such as housing conditions, but fail to provide deeper insights into the multidimensional nature of poverty. The Image data is more readily available in cities, but not regularly available for remote or rural areas. This representation of data may affect poverty predictions, and the literature lacks discussion on strategies to address this issue. Imagery factors like cloud cover, low resolution, and outdated images can significantly affect predictions, particularly in developing countries where access to high-resolution imagery is limited. Natural environmental features, such as vegetation or landscape, can influence the visual appearance of areas in ways which is not related to poverty. Models trained on image data from one region or time period are difficult to generalize to other regions or contexts. On the other hand, the literature that focuses on textual data, including living conditions measurement surveys or census data, lags in the frequency of data collection. These surveys take a long time for conduction and also for analyze. Thus, the data they provide is not real-time and does not guarantee correct predictions. This chapter aims to demonstrate an interdisciplinary approach drawn on expertise from data science, social sciences, and development studies, reflecting a holistic understanding of poverty as an outcome. In the context of multidimensional poverty assessment, integrating micro-level household data with macro-level census statistics offers a detailed view of socio-economic deprivation.

4.2 Scope of this chapter

By utilizing advanced feature engineering, machine learning algorithms, and multimodal analytical frameworks, this study seeks to derive fine-grained insights into the poverty landscape of Madhya Pradesh. The specific objectives of the research are as follows:

1. To identify the most relevant features from textual data for predicting poverty.
2. To design a deep learning based integrated framework for the predic-

tion of poverty in the Madhya Pradesh region of India, which will consider textual and satellite image features.

4.3 Dataset Description

4.3.1 Survey Data

We conducted a structured survey to form the dataset "Dataset Preparation for Prediction of poverty in Madhya Pradesh (India) region" © L-147127/2024 as mentioned in Chapter 3 which comprised of 45 questions across 50 districts in Madhya Pradesh, India. The questionnaire covered key aspects of household living conditions, including housing, health, education, electricity access, water availability, and community participation. Each household response was geo-tagged at the district level. The survey captured both binary and ordinal variables, providing micro-level insights into socioeconomic well-being.

4.3.2 Textual Dataset Compilation

The textual dataset for this study is derived from two primary sources: the 2011 Census of India, conducted by the Government of India [87], and the 2015–16 Demographic and Health Survey (DHS), which is publicly available [88]. The DHS provides an extensive range of socio-economic indicators at the district level in Madhya Pradesh, offering a comprehensive overview of demographic, economic, and infrastructural characteristics. Key variables include district identifiers, geographical area, urban–rural distribution, population density, sex ratio, literacy rates, employment statistics, housing conditions, and access to essential services. Data gathered from these official sources, when integrated with survey responses, enable robust statistical analysis and the inclusion of micro-level contextual details necessary for training poverty prediction models. This integration facilitates a more nuanced understanding of poverty dynamics and captures diverse socio-economic realities across Madhya Pradesh.

4.3.3 Data Merging and Preprocessing

We integrated the constructed dataset with census data by aligning both sources on the district column. Geographic alignment was carefully considered to ensure consistency between survey records and official census information.

- Households were matched to their respective districts using a geographic identifier, specifically the district name.
- Consistent naming conventions were enforced across survey and census datasets to avoid mismatches.
- The census data for Madhya Pradesh, obtained from official government records, included a wide range of attributes such as:
  - **Population statistics**: total population, sex ratio, and population density.
  - **Economic indicators**: workforce participation (main/marginal workers), employment types (cultivators, laborers), and non-working population.
  - **Literacy and urbanization**: literacy rate, projected population (2024), and urban–rural distribution.
  - **Infrastructure indicators**: houseless population and access-related indicators.

The integrated dataset was further refined through systematic cleaning:

- Metadata rows were removed, and the appropriate header row was set.
- District names were standardized by trimming spaces and converting all text to lowercase for uniformity.
- Non-numeric characters were eliminated from numerical fields, and missing values were treated appropriately.

This process ensured that the survey and census datasets were fully harmonized, providing a reliable foundation for subsequent poverty prediction modeling. The final merged dataset is in the form shown in Equation 4.1:

Let:

- $S_d = \{\bar{x}_1^d, \bar{x}_2^d, \ldots, \bar{x}_m^d\}$: aggregated survey features for district d,
- $C_d = \{c_1^d, c_2^d, \ldots, \bar{c}_k^d\}$: census features for district d.

Then the final merged feature vector is as given in Eq. 4.1 below:

$$F_d = S_d \cup C_d \tag{4.1}$$

This merged vector F_d represents the combined micro- and macro-level features and is used for poverty prediction modeling.

4.4 Feature Engineering and Extraction

After compiling the textual dataset, we performed feature engineering so as to create features which can derive meaningful insights for poverty prediction. This involved the creation of new features which can correlate with multidimensional nature of poverty in Madhya Pradesh.

Derived Indicators for Socio-Economic and Environmental Analysis

1. Population Growth Rate (PGR) is calculated as given in Eq. (4.2):

$$\text{PGR}(t) = \frac{P(t) - P(t-1)}{P(t-1)} \times 100 \tag{4.2}$$

Where:

- $\text{PGR}(t)$: Population Growth Rate at time t (in percentage)

Table 4.1: Source Data Attributes Used for Computing Derived Indicators

Derived Indicator	**Source Data Attributes**	**Data Source**
Population Growth Rate (PGR)	Total Population at time t and $t-1$	Census
Dependency Ratio (DR)	Non-Working Population, Total Engaged Workers	Census + Survey
Economic Activity Index (EAI)	Sector-wise worker counts (cultivators, labourers, industry, others)	Census
Employment Diversity (ED)	Sector-wise workers, Total Engaged Workers	Census
Infrastructure Score (IS)	Area under Urban Region, Urban Area Population, Population Density	Census
Living Conditions Index (LCI)	Sex Ratio, Literacy Rate, Houseless Population Ratio	Census + Survey
Environmental Sustainability Index (ESI)	Population Density, Non-Working Population, Total Population	Census

- PP(t): Projected Population Estimate at time t
- $P(t-1)$: Total Population at the previous time point $(t-1)$

2. Dependency Ratio (DR) is calculated as given in Eq. (4.3):

$$\text{DR} = \frac{\text{NW}}{\text{TEW}} \tag{4.3}$$

Where:

- NW: Non-Working Population (e.g., children, retired people)
- TEW: Total Engaged Workers (employed individuals)

3. Economic Activity Index (EAI) is calculated as given in Eq. (4.4):

$$\text{EAI}_d = \sum_{i=1}^{n_d} \text{Workers}_i \tag{4.4}$$

Where:

- Workers_i: Number of individuals working in sector i, including:

- Regular_Working_Cultivators
- Regular_Working_Agriculture_Labourer
- Regular_Working_Household_Industries
- Regular_Working_Other_Workers

4. Employment Diversity (ED) is calculated as given in Eq. (4.5):

$$\mathrm{ED}_d = \frac{\sum_{i=1}^{n_d} \mathrm{Workers}_i}{\mathrm{TEW}_d} \tag{4.5}$$

Where:

- ED: Employment Diversity Index
- $\mathrm{Workers}_i$: Individuals working in sector i
- TEW: Total Engaged Workers

5. Infrastructure Score (IS) is calculated as given in Eq. (4.6):

$$\mathrm{IS}_d = \frac{\mathrm{AU}_d + \mathrm{UAP}_d + \mathrm{PD}_d}{3} \tag{4.6}$$

Where:

- AU: Area under Urban Region
- UAP: Urban Area Population
- PD: Population Density

6.Living Conditions Index (LCI) is calculated as given in Eq. (4.7):

$$\mathrm{LCI}_d = \frac{\mathrm{SR}_d + \mathrm{LR}_d + \mathrm{HPR}_d}{3} \tag{4.7}$$

Where:

- SR: Average Sex Ratio
- LR: Literacy Rate
- HP Ratio: Houseless Population Ratio

7. Environmental Sustainability Index (ESI) is calculated as given in Eq. (4.8):

$$\mathrm{ESI}_d = \frac{\mathrm{PD}_d}{\mathrm{NW}_d/\mathrm{TP}_d} = \frac{\mathrm{PD}_d\,\mathrm{TP}_d}{\mathrm{NW}_d} \tag{4.8}$$

Where:

- PD: Population Density
- NW: Non-Working Population
- TP: Total Population

These features collectively contribute to a better understanding of poverty dynamics, enabling informed decision-making and facilitating targeted interventions for poverty alleviation.

4.5 Image Dataset Description

In addition to textual data, a key component of this study involved the use of visual data in the form of satellite imagery. The images were sourced from Google Earth Imagery (GE) [109], acquired in 2019, and consist of three-band multispectral data with a spatial resolution of approximately 4.09 meters. These bands correspond to the red, green, and blue (RGB) wavelengths, providing high-quality true-color representations of the study area. Google Earth imagery integrates data from multiple satellite sources, combining lower-resolution inputs from NASA's Land-

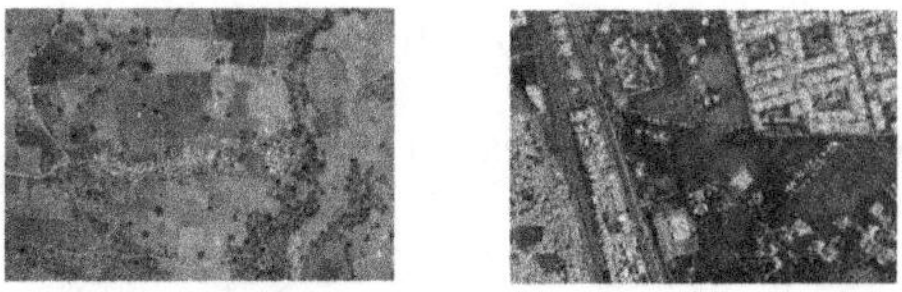

Figure 4.1: Poor and non-Poor areas images from the dataset, taken from Google Earth Engine

sat program with higher-resolution imagery contributed by the European Space Agency's Sentinel missions, Maxar Technologies' WorldView series, and Airbus' SPOT and Pleiades satellites.

A total of 1,577 images were collected and manually annotated into two categories: poor areas and non-poor areas, as shown in Figure 4.1, to ensure representation of the diverse socio-economic conditions in different regions of Madhya Pradesh. The features extracted from these images were later integrated with the textual data set to enable a multimodal framework for predicting poverty.

To enhance the diversity of the data set and prevent overfitting during model training, standard data augmentation techniques such as rotation, flipping, scaling, and translation were applied. After augmentation, the data set expanded significantly, resulting in a larger pool of training samples that improved the robustness of feature learning.

4.5.1 Preprocessing of Image dataset

The preprocessing of satellite imagery is a crucial step in ensuring that the visual data set is consistent, standardized, and ready for feature extraction through deep learning models. Since raw satellite images often vary in resolution, quality, and orientation, systematic preprocessing was carried out to make them compatible with the VGG16 architecture. This included resizing all images to a fixed dimension of 224 × 224 pixels, normalizing pixel intensity values to stabilize model training, and carefully inspecting the data set to remove corrupted or low-contrast patches. These steps ensured that the visual inputs were uniform, reliable, and representative, thereby enhancing the robustness of subsequent feature extraction and classification.

4.5.1.1 Resizing

All images were resized to 224×224 pixels to conform to the input specifications of the VGG16 architecture. Figure 4.2 presents the original image, while Figure 4.3 illustrates the resized version used as input for the model.

Figure 4.2: Original Image

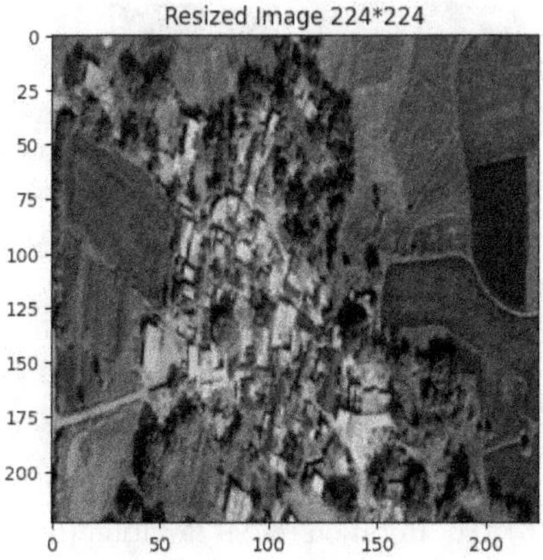

Figure 4.3: Resized Image

4.5.1.2 Normalization

Pixel intensity values were then normalized as shown in Eq. 4.9 to ensure uniformity and to facilitate faster model convergence during training. The normalization was applied as:

$$I'_{ij} = \frac{I_{ij} - \mu}{\sigma} \tag{4.9}$$

Where:

- I_{ij} = original pixel intensity at position (i, j),
- μ = mean pixel intensity of the image (or dataset),
- σ = standard deviation of pixel intensities,
- I'_{ij} = normalized pixel value.

This standard *z-score normalization* ensures that pixel values are centered around zero with unit variance, making the input more stable for deep learning.

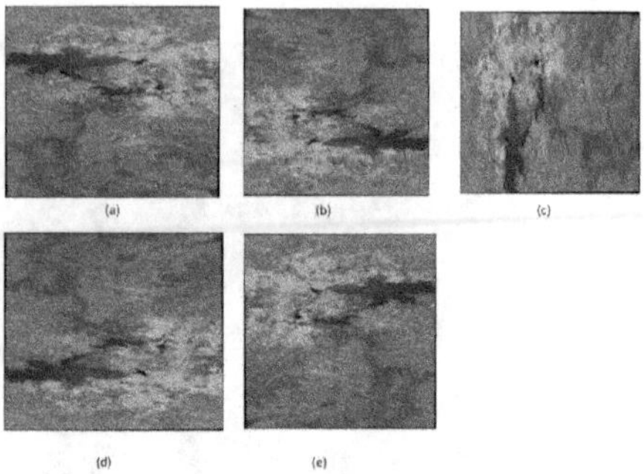

Figure 4.4: Augmentation on Image
(a)Original Image (b) 180° Rotation (c) 90°Rotation (d)Vertical flip (e) Horizontal flip

4.5.1.3 Augmentation

To artificially expand the data set and improve the generalization of the model, augmentation techniques were used. This step increased image diversity, mimicked different viewing conditions, and reduced overfitting. The following transformations were applied:

- Rotation: 90° and 180° rotations to handle variations in image orientation.
- Flipping: Horizontal and vertical flips to simulate alternate perspectives of the same area.

Through augmentation, the data set expanded substantially as shown in Figure 4.4, creating multiple transformed variants of each original image. This ensured that the model was exposed to a richer set of training examples, strengthening its robustness in identifying poverty-related visual cues.

4.6 Proposed Model Architecture

Our proposed predictive models for poverty prediction, which integrate textual and visual data sources, are described in the sections given below :

4.6.1 Proposed Model for textual data analysis

To extract relevant features from the textual dataset, such as Population Growth Rate, Dependency Ratio, Economic Activity Index, Employment Diversity, Infrastructure Score, Living Conditions Index, and Environmental Sustainability Index we applied feature engineering by combining and assessing the features. These features serve as inputs to our predictive models and capture key socio-economic dimensions of poverty.

4.6.2 Proposed Model for Visual Data Analysis

To analyze the image data, we used a pre-trained VGG16 convolutional neural network [90] (CNN) model for feature extraction. VGG16, originally trained on the ImageNet dataset [91], is a deep learning architecture used for image feature extraction tasks. It extracts high-level features from images. Our goal is to utilize these features for socioeconomic analysis and urban infrastructure assessment. VGG16 has an architecture with 16 layers; the input layer takes an image of 224*224 and is followed by convolution layers and max pooling layers, which are then followed by two fully connected layers with ReLU activation function. Then comes an output layer with a softmax activation function. Figure 4.5, shows the overview of the architecture of VGG 16. The layers extract features at different levels of extraction.

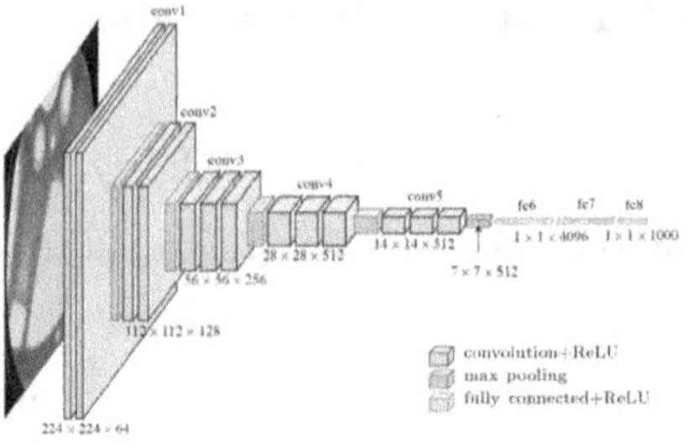

Figure 4.5: VGG16 architecture used for feature extraction.

[92]

The following steps outline the feature extraction process through VGG16:

1. The VGG16 model with pre-trained weights from ImageNet [93], a large-scale dataset consisting of millions of labelled images across 1,000 object categories is loaded. We specifically excluded the top fully connected layers to extract high-level convolutional features instead of final classification outputs. This allows us to capture meaningful image patterns while by not taking into account the object detection classes designed for ImageNet classification.

2. The input images were pre-processed to make it compatible with VGG16 model. This involved sub steps:

   - Resizing: 1577 images were loaded using the OpenCV library and converted from TIFF format to RGB, as required by the VGG16 model. The image was then resized to 224x224 pixels, which is the standard input size for VGG16.

   - Batch Dimension Addition: Since the VGG16 model expects input in batches, a new dimension was added to the image array, transforming it into a 4D array with the shape (1577, 224, 224,3).

- Data Augmentation was performed to increase the size of dataset by rotation. Noisy images were discarded.

3. After pre-processing, the images data was given as input to VGG16 model to extract features. The fully connected layers were excluded, the output of the model gives the feature maps from the last convolutional block. These feature maps encapsulate high-level patterns in the image, such as shapes, textures, and semantic content that are critical for further analysis. The shape of the output feature map was (1577, 25088)

4. The 3D feature map was flattened into a 1D vector.

5. The extracted and flattened feature vector was saved for further analysis.

4.6.3 Textual and Image Feature Merging Description

The proposed multimodal framework integrates information from three complementary data sources: (i) satellite imagery, (ii) household survey data, and (iii) official census statistics. While the household survey comprised 45 questions capturing detailed socioeconomic, infrastructural, and environmental aspects, not all raw survey responses were directly merged with visual features. To ensure compatibility with district-level satellite imagery and census data, household-level responses were first aggregated at the district level and transformed into representative indicators as shown in Table 4.2.

Census data provided authoritative district-level demographic and population statistics, which were directly incorporated without aggregation. Survey data and census data together were used to derive composite indicators reflecting population structure, economic activity, living conditions, infrastructure availability, and environmental sustainability. Only these derived district-level attributes were merged with image-based features extracted from satellite imagery to form the final multimodal feature set.

This strategy ensured spatial consistency across data sources, reduced dimensionality, and enabled effective fusion of visual and non-visual information for poverty classification.

Table 4.2: Data Attributes Used for Multimodal Feature Fusion

Data Source	Attributes Used for Fusion	Level
Census Data	Total Population, Population Density, Sex Ratio, Urban Area Population, Rural Area Population, Population Growth Rate	District
Household Survey (Aggregated)	Poverty Rate, Economic Activity Index, Employment Diversity, Dependency Ratio, Infrastructure Score, Living Conditions Index, Environmental Sustainability Index, Poverty Class	District
Satellite Imagery	Deep visual features extracted using CNN architectures (VGG16)	District

4.6.4 Dataset Splitting for Training and Testing

The merged dataset, which combines textual features (survey and census data) with visual features extracted from VGG16 (early fusion), was divided into training and testing subsets. This division ensures that the model is trained on a majority of the data while being evaluated on an independent, unseen portion for performance validation. Out of a total of 7,785 images, 6,228 images (80%) were allocated for training, and 1,557 images (20%) were reserved for testing.

This standard 80:20 split strategy allows the proposed model to learn representative feature patterns during training while ensuring that evaluation metrics reflect its ability to generalize to new data.

4.7 Proposed Integrated Model

We employed a multimodal fusion approach to merge textual and visual data streams, combining features extracted from textual and visual datasets into a unified feature representation. This integrated feature representation was fed into machine learning models Support Vector Machine [94] and Random Forest [95], for poverty prediction, which is then compared with our proposed Fusion model which is a sequential neural network model with three layers. The proposed algorithm is as follows:

Input: Image Dataset = `ImageData`, Text Dataset = `TextData`

Step 1: Data Preprocessing

- Load `ImageData`
- Resize to 224x224 pixels
- Normalize as per VGG16 requirements
- Apply augmentation (zoom, rotation)
- Load `TextData`
- Perform feature engineering (create relevant features, drop unnecessary)

Step 2: Feature Extraction

- Load pre-trained VGG16 model (without top layer)
- Pass `ImageData` through VGG16 to extract features

Step 3: Merge Datasets

- CNN-derived image feature embeddings and engineered socioeconomic feature vectors are combined using feature-level concatenation to construct the unified multimodal feature matrix (MergedDataset) used for model training.

Step 4: Model Training

- Split `MergedDataset` into training and validation sets
- Define a fusion model with:
  - Input layer for image features
  - Input layer for text features
  - Dense Layer 1: 64 neurons, ReLU
  - Dense Layer 2: 32 neurons, ReLU
  - Dense Layer 3: 1 neuron, Sigmoid
- Compile model (Binary Cross-Entropy, Adam optimizer)
- Train and validate the model

Step 5: Prediction

- Load new image and text data
- Preprocess and extract features
- Concatenate to form `NewCombinedFeatures`
- Predict poverty labels using trained model

Step 6: Output

- Apply Random Forest and SVM for comparison
- Output predictions indicating poverty areas

End

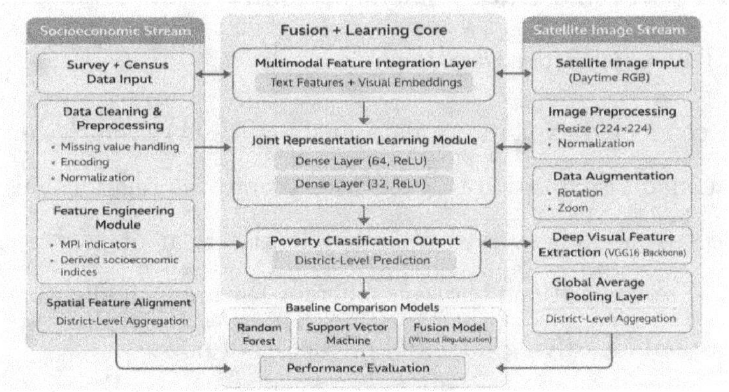

Figure 4.6: The proposed multimodal poverty prediction framework.

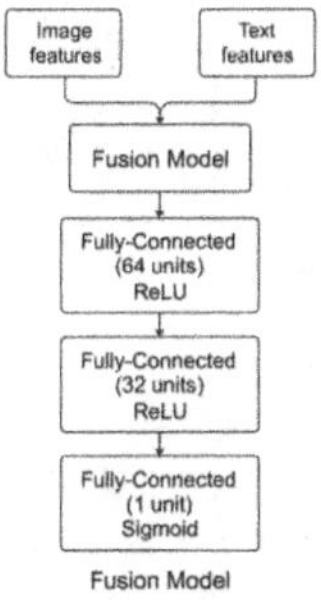

Parameter	Value
Dense Layer 1 Units	64
Dense Layer 1 Activation	ReLU
Dense Layer 2 Units	32
Dense Layer 2 Activation	ReLU
Output Units (Classification)	1
Output Activation Function	Sigmoid
Loss Function	Binary Cross-Entropy
Optimizer	Adam
Learning Rate	0.001
Batch Size	64
Epochs	10

Figure 4.7: Hyperparameters and architectural details of the proposed Fusion model

Figure 4.6 shows the Integrated Model Architecture, and Figure 4.7 shows the details of hyperparameters for combining textual and VGG16-extracted image features.

4.8 Results

In this section, we present the results of our analysis and discuss the implications for the prediction of poverty in Madhya Pradesh.

4.8.1 Textual Data Analysis Results

4.8.1.1 Exploratory Data Analysis

We conducted exploratory data analysis (EDA) using techniques such as heat map visualization to gain insights into the relationships between socioeconomic indicators and poverty levels. Heat maps were generated to visualize correlations between different features, highlighting key associations and identifying potential predictors of poverty.

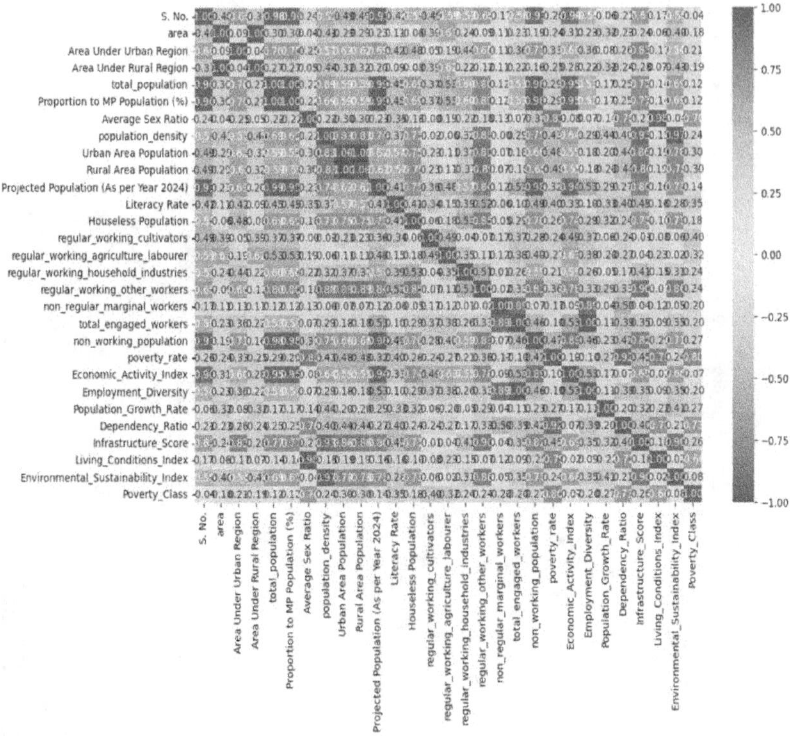

Figure 4.8: Heat map displaying the relationships between various socio-economic, demographic, and environmental indicators

We analyzed the 'Poverty Rate' for the indicators of poverty, looking for correlations with factors. The adjacent column of the heat map in Figure 4.8 shows that Non-Working Population, Employment Diversity and high dependency ratio are highly correlated with high poverty rates. The areas which are having higher non-working population are prone towards poverty, also areas high dependency ratio fall under poor areas.

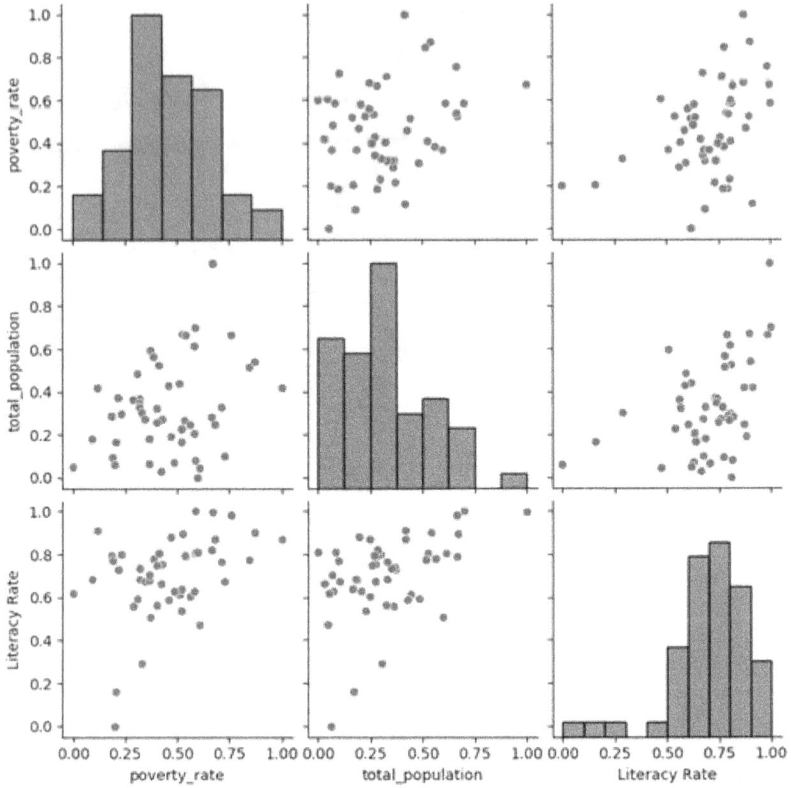

Figure 4.9: Pairwise scatter plot matrix with histograms shows relationships between poverty rate, total population, and literacy rate across different districts

Figure 4.9 and Figure 4.10 shows the distributions and interrelationships among poverty rate, total population, and literacy rate at the district level. The scatter plot matrix shows the relationships between three variables: poverty rate, total population, and literacy rate. The scatter plots reveal that there is a slight negative correlation between poverty rate and literacy rate regions with higher literacy rates give lower poverty rates.There does not appear to be a strong correlation between total population and poverty rate or total population and literacy rate, indicating that population size may not impact these two variables in this dataset. This observation supports the need for a multidimensional approach to poverty prediction rather than reliance on population size alone.

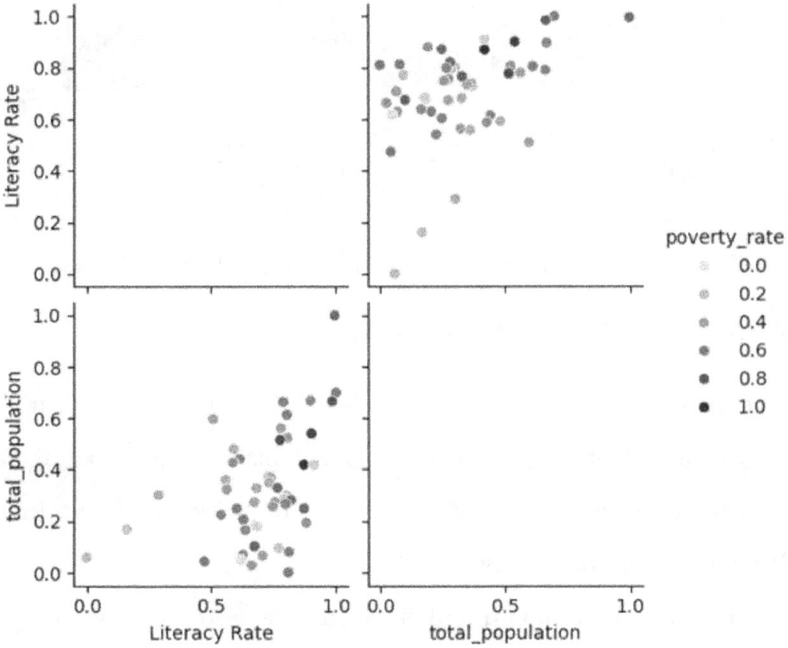

Figure 4.10: Scatter plot matrix shows the relationships between literacy rate, total population, and poverty rate

Figure 4.11 showsa box plot figure which illustrates the distribution and variability of the prominent socioeconomic features used in poverty modeling. The figure presents the spread, median, interquartile range, and outliers for key engineered indicators, including poverty rate, economic activity index, infrastructure score, living conditions index, dependency ratio, non-working population, and population density.

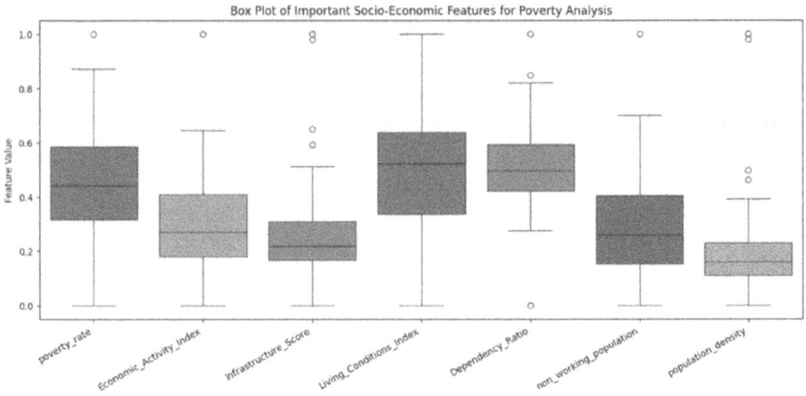

Figure 4.11: Box Plot of Important Socioeconomic Features for Poverty Analysis

4.8.2 Visual Data Analysis Results

The visual data analysis using the VGG16 Convolutional Neural Network (CNN) architecture provided additional insights into spatial patterns of poverty in Madhya Pradesh. Figure 4.11 shows an Input Image of the Bhopal district of Madhya Pradesh.

Feature Extraction: In our study, we used the VGG16 convolutional neural network (CNN) to extract deep features from daytime satellite imagery, which was then integrated into our poverty prediction model. The VGG16 model, pre-trained on the ImageNet dataset gives us the ability to identify complex visual patterns and features across varying landscapes.

Figure 4.12: Input Image of Huzur, Bhopal, Madhya Pradesh, India

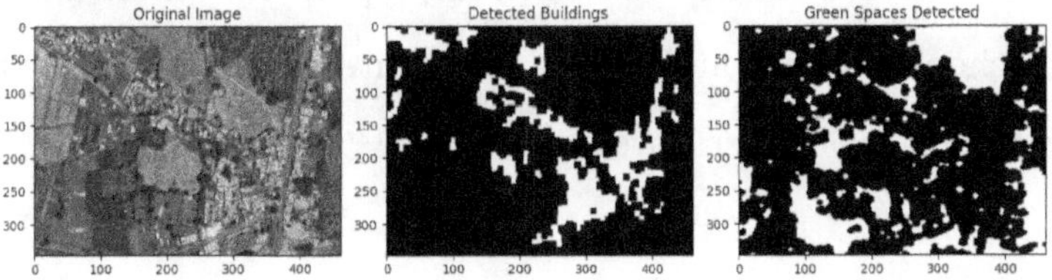

Figure 4.13: Feature map visualization from VGG 16

The features extracted from the satellite images, as shown in Figure 4.12, included:

1. **Infrastructure density:** VGG16 identified features of built-up areas, such as buildings, roads, bridges, and industrial zones. These features correlate with higher economic activity and better access to services, indicating lower poverty levels.

2. **Agricultural Land:** The model was able to classify agricultural areas and barren land. A higher proportion of barren land corresponds to higher poverty rates, while districts with well-managed agricultural lands showed lower poverty indicators.

3. **Vegetation Coverage:** The amount of forest or vegetation cover is another visual feature extracted by VGG16. In rural areas, the presence of forest or green cover was associated with lower poverty levels due to the involvement of the local population in natural resources for livelihoods. Figure 4.13 shows the Pseudo-NDVI (Simulated Vegetation Index) map derived from satellite im- agery.However, deforested land often indicates economic challenges.

4. **Infrastructure Quality:** In addition to identifying built-up areas, the model captured the quality of infrastructure, such as the presence of well-maintained roads, housing types, and visible amenities such as schools and hospitals. This contributed significantly to the prediction of higher or lower poverty levels.

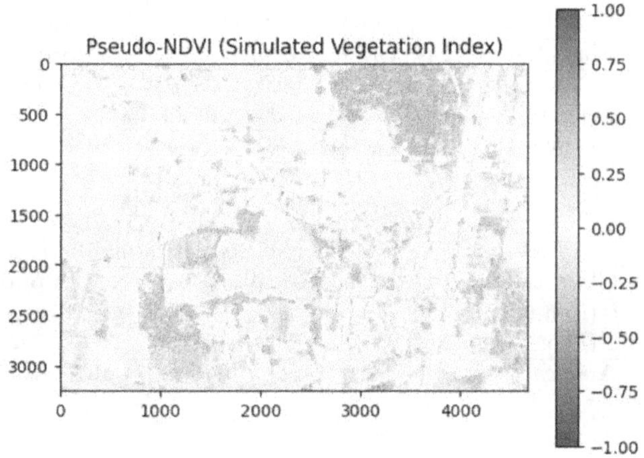

Figure 4.14: Pseudo-NDVI (Simulated Vegetation Index) map derived from satellite imagery.

4.8.3 Predictive Performance

Proposed integrated model, which combined textual and visual dataset features, shows better predictive performance compared to models trained on individual data sources. By providing strengths of textual and visual data for analysis, we achieved higher accuracy in poverty prediction. We applied Random Forest Classifier, SVM classifier, along with the Proposed Fusion model and the Proposed Fusion Model with regularization, and the following are the results. Table 4.3 shows the performance of the Random Forest Classifier, Table 4.4 shows the SVM Performance, Table 4.5 and Table 4.6 display the performance of the Fusion model and with regularization, respectively.

Table 4.3: Random Forest Classifier Performance

Class Label	**Precision**	**Recall**	**F1**	**Support**
0 (Non-Poor)	0.93	0.92	0.92	785
1 (Poor)	0.94	0.94	0.94	792
Accuracy:				**93.10% (1,577 total)**

Table 4.4: Support Vector Machine (SVM) Performance

Class Label	Precision	Recall	F1	Support
0 (Non-Poor)	0.91	0.90	0.90	785
1 (Poor)	0.92	0.93	0.92	792
Accuracy:				**91.50% (1,577 total)**

Table 4.5: Fusion Model (No Regularization) Performance

Class Label	Precision	Recall	F1	Support
0 (Non-Poor)	0.94	0.93	0.93	785
1 (Poor)	0.95	0.96	0.95	792
Accuracy:				**94.40% (1,577 total)**

Table 4.6: Fusion Model (With Regularization) Performance

Class Label	Precision	Recall	F1	Support
0 (Non-Poor)	0.92	0.91	0.91	785
1 (Poor)	0.93	0.94	0.93	792
Accuracy:				**92.20% (1,577 total)**

The results show consistently high and well-balanced precision and recall across both classes, indicating no systematic bias toward Non-Poor or Poor. With nearly balanced support (785 vs. 792). Random Forest is a strong baseline (93.1% accuracy; F1 0.92–0.94), SVM trails slightly (91.5% accuracy; F1 0.90–0.92), and the Fusion model without regularization performs best (94.4% accuracy; F1 0.95; AUC 0.97). The Fusion model with regularization is modestly lower (92.2% accuracy; F1 0.93), reflecting the usual bias–variance trade-off and potentially greater robustness. For poverty prediction, recall for the Poor class is most critical: the fusion model without regularization attains a recall of 0.96, implying very few missed Poor households, while maintaining high precision (0.95).

Table 4.7: Performance comparison of models

Model	Accuracy (%)	F1 Score	AUC
Random Forest	93.10	0.94	0.96
SVM	91.50	0.90	0.96
Proposed Fusion Model (No Regularization)	**94.40**	**0.95**	**0.97**
Proposed Fusion Model (With Regularization)	92.20	0.93	0.96

Table 4.8: Confusion Matrix-Random Forest Classifier

Actual / Predicted	Non-Poor (0)	Poor (1)
Non-Poor (0)	722	63
Poor (1)	48	744

Table 4.9: Confusion Matrix-SVM Classifier

Actual / Predicted	Non-Poor (0)	Poor (1)
Non-Poor (0)	707	78
Poor (1)	55	737

Table 4.10: Confusion Matrix-Fusion Model (No Regularization)

Actual / Predicted	Non-Poor (0)	Poor (1)
Non-Poor (0)	730	55
Poor (1)	32	760

Table 4.11: Confusion Matrix-Fusion Model (With Regularization)

Actual / Predicted	Non-Poor (0)	Poor (1)
Non-Poor (0)	714	71
Poor (1)	48	744

The confusion matrices in Tables 4.8 to 4.11 validate the tabular metrics. Off-diagonal counts are lowest for the Proposed Fusion model, followed by Random Forest, then SVM. Finally, because class supports are balanced, the summary accuracy and F1 in the comparison table align with the per-class scores; the high AUC (0.96–0.97) across models confirms strong separability, with the Fusion model providing the best overall discrimination and the Random Forest remaining a robust baseline.

4.9 Performance Analysis

Proposed Fusion Model outperforms Random Forest and SVM methods in terms of classification accuracy, Recall and Precision values and Overall F1 score. Comparative analysis of various models is done in Table 4.7. This approach enabled the development of predictive models that effectively defines the complex details of socio-economic factors influencing poverty levels across different districts of state. Through the integration of textual and visual data, the predictive models could utilize both datasets' strengths.

While textual data provided comprehensive statistical information and contextual details, visual data offered detailed and spatial information about the physical environment. By combining these sources of information, the models could generate more accurate predictions of poverty within Madhya Pradesh. While we achieve high accuracy with our proposed model in predicting poverty using visual data, there are limitations that must be considered. These challenges define the complexities of incorporating many dimensions of poverty and suggest ways for improving model performance in future research. Satellite images have limitations in showing social and cultural factors that affect poverty. They may fail to capture temporary issues like seasonal poverty during droughts or failed harvests in rural areas or migration during conditions like COVID-19, which can lead to biased predictions. Future models should use data from sources like social media and E-commerce to capture a better picture of poverty. Using time-series data can help models find overall shifts in poverty throughout the year. In diverse countries like India, models trained in one region may not work well in another due to differences in infrastructure and social conditions. For example, poverty looks different in Madhya Pradesh compared to that in Kerala. Kerala, where there is more green area as compared to the infrastructural development in Madhya Pradesh or other states, which, according to our model is one of the important factor while analysing a region for poverty. Using transfer learning to adapt models for specific areas can improve their accuracy. Testing models in various geographic and socioeconomic contexts can also ensure they are effective across different situations.

4.10 Discussion

While our model provides analytical insights into poverty patterns in Madhya Pradesh, it is important to correlate these findings within the internal socio-political status of the state. Several key factors provide these insights:

1. **Caste dynamics:** The Social caste system plays a major role in economic opportunities and access to resources. For example, scheduled castes and scheduled tribes, who make up 36.10% of the state's population, often face difficulty in accessing quality education, healthcare, and employment opportunities. Our model's findings on education and employment should be interpreted with this social reality in mind.

2. **Political landscape:** Madhya Pradesh has alternating governance between two major political parties, each with different approaches to poverty reduction. Policy continuity between states significantly impacts the long-term effectiveness of anti-poverty programs.

3. **Rural-urban divide:** Madhya Pradesh has a predominantly rural population; the rate of urbanization is slower as compared to some other Indian states. This rural-urban divide reflects differences in infrastructure, economic opportunities, and access to services. Our model's focus on infrastructure as a poverty predictor should be understood within this context of uneven development.

4. **Tribal rights and forest management:** With one of the largest tribal populations in India, Madhya Pradesh faces unique challenges in balancing tribal rights, forest conservation, and economic development. Policies for the Forest Rights have a major role in poverty among tribal communities, many of whom depend on forest resources for their livelihoods.

5. **Gender disparities:** While our model does not focus on gender-based factors, it's important to recognize that women in Madhya Pradesh face additional barriers in education, employment, and access to resources. Programs aimed at women's empowerment, such as Ladli laxmi and Ladli Behna can have a major impact on poverty reduction at the household level.

6. **Historical context:** The current poverty patterns in Madhya Pradesh

are also result of historical factors, including the legacy of the princely states that once made up this region, land ownership patterns established during colonial rule, and post-independence development policies.

Considering these socio-political factors, our findings on poverty predictions will have new dimensions. For example, the relationship between infrastructure quality and poverty levels is not only a matter of physical development, but also reflects historical investment patterns, political priorities, and the challenges of implementing large-scale projects in socially complex environments. Similarly, while our model identifies education as a key factor in poverty reduction, the reality on the ground is more complicated. Access to quality education is impacted by caste identities, gender roles, and the rural-urban divide. Therefore, policy-making based on our findings must be framed to address these underlying social dynamics.

4.11 Summary

In this study, we have analyzed poverty prediction in Madhya Pradesh, using both textual and visual data analysis techniques. Through feature engineering, extraction, and integrated modelling. Our innovative multi-modal approach, combining image analysis and textual data, has provided new insights into poverty patterns across Madhya Pradesh. By using both visual and textual information, we have identified indicators that can be the predictors of poverty with a level of analysis that traditional methods often miss. Based on these findings, we propose the following actionable recommendations for policymakers:

1. **Targeted Infrastructure Development:** The Proposed analysis highlighted infrastructure quality as a strong predictor of poverty levels. We recommend: a) Focusing on road construction and improvement in identified poor areas, particularly focusing on connectivity to remote villages. b) Upgrading schools and healthcare facilities in

vulnerable regions. c) Expanding rural electrification efforts, with a focus on regions where our model indicated low industrial areas.

2. **Education-Focused Interventions:** Textual data analysis shows a strong correlation between education levels and poverty. We suggest: a) Starting scholarship programs for students in identified poor districts, with a special focus on girls' education. b) Implementing online learning initiatives in areas where physical access to schools is limited like night school under Rashtriya Saksharta Mission c) Developing adult literacy programs considering specific needs of different regions, as indicated by poverty predictions d) Focusing on Skill development programs for rural areas to make the people employable e) Schemes like Mid-day meals that is providing free food to students in schools should be taken more into consideration

3. **Employment Generation:** Our proposed model identified unemployment as a key contributor to poverty. We recommend: a) Expanding and optimizing the implementation of MGNREGA (The Mahatma Gandhi National Rural Employment Guarantee Act) [96] by Indian government in districts flagged as high-poverty areas by our model. b) Developing skill training programs for economic potential of different regions, as given by our image and textual data analysis for example Indore and nearby places have lot of mechanical industries and place near Panna district has diamond ores, so focusing on those training programs can be developed c) Promoting Entrepreneurship in areas where our model indicates high poverty but also potential for economic activity.

4. **Agricultural Support:** Image analysis of crop patterns and land use provided insights into agricultural challenges. We propose: a) Implementing crop diversification programs in regions where lower yield due to repetitive farming is factor for poverty. b) Expanding irrigation infrastructure in drought-prone areas identified through our satellite

imagery analysis. c) Introducing climate-friendly farming techniques in regions where our model indicates high vulnerability to environmental conditions.

5. **Technology-based monitoring:** Leveraging the power of our multimodal approach, we suggest: a) Developing a real-time poverty monitoring system that uses satellite imagery and regularly updated textual data to track changes in poverty indicators. b) Creating a dashboard for policymakers that visualises the poverty predictions and allows for data-driven decision-making in resource allocation.

Through these insights provided by our multimodal poverty prediction model, policymakers will be able to design more effective, targeted, and efficient poverty alleviation strategies. This data-driven approach allows for a more detailed understanding of poverty dynamics in Madhya Pradesh and provides an outline that can make a difference in the lives of the state's most vulnerable populations.

Furthermore, we propose that this multimodal approach be expanded and refined for application in other states and at the national level. By continuously integrating new data sources and refining our algorithms, we can create a powerful tool for dynamic poverty mapping and intervention planning across India.

Chapter 5

Poverty Prediction using Nighttime Imagery with Environmental Indicators (AQI and Radiance)

This study focuses on finding techniques that help in accurately predicting poverty in a place so that appropriate steps could be taken to eradicate it and formulate targeted policies for the particular place. In Chapter 4, a multimodal integration of survey, daytime satellite images, and census data was proposed for prediction, which resulted in an accurate and efficient method. Along with the socio-economic analysis of a particular place, environmental data sources play a very important role in defining the economic status of the people living in that region. Environmental data sources have emerged as a powerful approach to address the limitations of traditional poverty measurement methods. In recent years, the Air Quality Index (AQI) has risen beyond expected thresholds, intensifying concerns about environmental justice. The persistent linkage between poverty and deteriorating air quality remains a central issue in this discourse. Research presented in Chapter 2 strongly supports the idea that pollution disproportionately impacts poor communities. Populations residing in environmentally stressed areas exhibit heightened vulnerability to ecological hazards due to limited access to clean air, water, and other essential resources. These disadvantages result in disproportionately adverse health outcomes. Pollution-related health disparities tend to intensify existing socioeconomic inequities, creating a reinforcing cycle of ill health and poverty. Exposure to environmental pollutants such as lead and particulate matter adversely affects children's cognitive development and academic performance, thereby constraining their future economic prospects. Among adults, the prevalence of pollution-induced illnesses contributes to increased healthcare expenditures and diminished productivity, further exacerbating financial hardship within these already resource-constrained communities.

Night-time light (NTL) imagery serves as a widely recognized proxy for economic growth, urbanization, and overall human activity. Although indirect, NTL data provide valuable information on levels of well-being, infrastructure development, and access to resources key dimensions of human progress captured through nocturnal illumination. Remote sensing technologies, particularly satellite-based observations from instruments such as the Visible Infrared Imaging Radiometer Suite (VIIRS), offer a spatially consistent and comprehensive means to evaluate patterns of human settlement, economic activity, and developmental disparities across regions. When these image-based indicators are combined with environmental parameters such as the Air Quality Index (AQI) and radiance intensity, it becomes possible to capture both the physical aspects of poverty and the environmental conditions that often correlate with socio-economic deprivation. This integrated data-driven framework enhances both the spatial and temporal resolution of poverty prediction models, making them more scalable, adaptive, and responsive to real-world dynamics. As a result, the fusion of satellite-derived features and environmental metrics enables more accurate and actionable poverty assessments, supporting evidence-based policy formulation and targeted interventions in line with sustainable development goals. This chapter will present a novel framework for poverty prediction that uses satellite-derived nighttime light (NTL) data alongside key environmental indicators, namely the Air Quality Index (AQI) and radiance intensity.

Nighttime light imagery, captured by instruments such as the Visible Infrared Imaging Radiometer Suite (VIIRS), provides a proxy for human activity, infrastructure development, and economic vibrancy. The spatial distribution and brightness of these lights are strongly correlated with socioeconomic indicators, making them a valuable source for poverty estimation. In parallel, environmental stressors such as poor air quality and low radiance levels have been increasingly linked to impoverished living conditions, particularly in urban slums and underserved rural areas.

The objective of this chapter is to build and validate a computational model that integrates features extracted from nighttime satellite imagery with AQI and radiance data to predict poverty levels across districts. By combining visual features using deep learning techniques (such as SENet or VGG16) with environmental statistics, the model aims to generate a more holistic and scalable measure of poverty likelihood. This multi-modal approach not only enhances prediction accuracy but also facilitates a deeper understanding of the spatial and environmental dynamics of poverty.

Figure 5.1: Administrative District Boundaries of Madhya Pradesh, India

5.1 Study Area and Dataset

As this study concentrates on the state of Madhya Pradesh, India, the most recent district-level datasets have been utilized for comprehensive analysis. Figure 5.1 depicts the 50 districts that delineate the administrative boundaries of the state. Geographically, Madhya Pradesh is situated at the heart of India, occupying a central position on the subcontinent. It is the second-largest state by area and the fifth-largest by population, encompassing a diverse range of ecological, cultural, and economic environments. The state's economy is predominantly agrarian, with a substantial portion of the population engaged in primary sector activities, particularly in rural districts. In contrast, urban centres such as Bhopal, Indore, Jabalpur, and Gwalior have witnessed significant industrial growth and expansion of service-oriented sectors in recent years.

5.2 Data Collection

An integrated multiple-source dataset, as shown in Figure 5.2, is formed for the analysis, covering environmental, geospatial and multi-dimensional indicators.

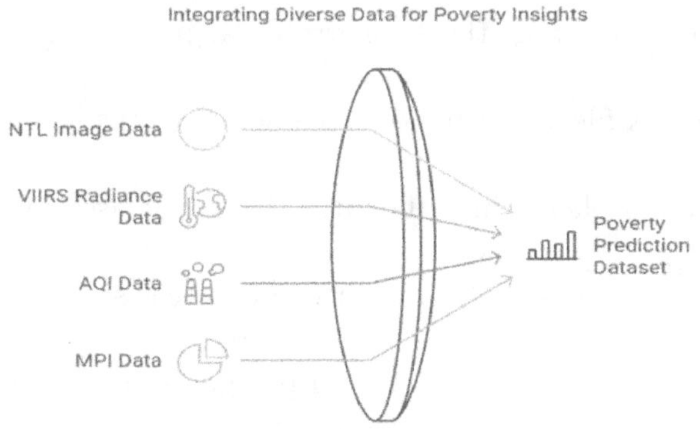

Figure 5.2: Integration of Multiple Data Sources for the Poverty Prediction Model

5.2.1 Nighttime Images

The acquisition of nighttime imagery necessitates well-defined regional boundaries. Accordingly, shapefiles defining the district boundaries of Madhya Pradesh were obtained from the official Geographic Information System (GIS) repository of the state for use in spatial filtering and analysis [97]. Shape files are a vector geospatial data format developed by Esri [98] to represent geographic features and their associated attributes. In the context of this study, shape files serve as the foundational spatial data structure for delineating administrative boundaries, specifically district-level boundaries within the state of Madhya Pradesh, India. These boundaries are essential for georeferencing and spatial alignment of the various datasets used in the poverty prediction model, including satellite imagery, environmental indicators, and survey data.

A typical shapefile consists of multiple component files that work together to represent both geometry and attribute data. The core components include:

- .shp – containing the geometry data (points, lines, polygons)
- an index file that enables rapid access to the geometry
- a tabular file storing attribute information associated with each shape
- optional files such as .prj for coordinate system metadata.

For this research, district-level polygon shapefiles were used to mask, extract and aggregate spatial information from raster datasets, including night-time light images and environmental layers. These shapefiles allowed for the spatial linkage of different data modalities, facilitating district-wise feature extraction and subsequent analysis. The use of shapefiles ensures consistency in the spatial resolution of the study and enables integration with Geographic Information System (GIS) tools [99] and platforms such as QGIS [100]and Google Earth Engine (GEE) [101]. Moreover, these shapefiles provided the spatial boundaries necessary to match and merge census data, survey responses, and satellite-derived features on a common geospatial reference frame.

Shapefiles were imported as an asset into Google Earth Engine (GEE) to clip the VIIRS raster dataset [102] for the study region. A zonal statistics approach was applied to compute district-wise aggregated nighttime light metrics. The extracted values were exported in Geo TIFF format.

The night-time light (NTL) brightness data utilized in this study were obtained from the Visible Infrared Imaging Radiometer Suite (VIIRS) Day/Night Band (DNB) sensor aboard the Suomi National Polar-orbiting Partnership (Suomi NPP) satellite [103], operated by the National Oceanic and Atmospheric Administration (NOAA) [104]. The dataset was accessed through the Google Earth Engine (GEE) platform for further processing and analysis.

The VIIRS Day/Night Band (DNB) sensor records radiance values within the 500–900 nm spectral range, providing enhanced radiometric sensitivity, minimized saturation effects, and finer spatial resolution (500 m per pixel at nadir) compared to its predecessor, the Defence Meteorological Satellite Program's Operational Linescan System (DMSP-OLS). The dataset includes daily, monthly, and annual composites, facilitating temporal assessments of artificial illumination and human activity patterns. The VIIRS NTL dataset was selected for this study owing to its superior spatial and temporal resolution, advanced radiometric calibration, and demonstrated effectiveness as a reliable proxy for economic activity, urbanization, and electrification levels. Given the significant correlation between NTL brightness and infrastructure development, this dataset provides a valuable tool for monitoring urbanization, economic disparities, and sustainable development trends across Madhya Pradesh's districts. Figure 5.3 is NTL image of the Ashok Nagar district located in Madhya Pradesh, with the boundary given by the shape file. Figure 5.4 shows the Google Earth Engine code platform through which these satellite images are downloaded, giving a specific time range.

Figure 5.3: Overlay of Nighttime Light Imagery with Administrative Boundaries of Ashoknagar District, Madhya Pradesh, India

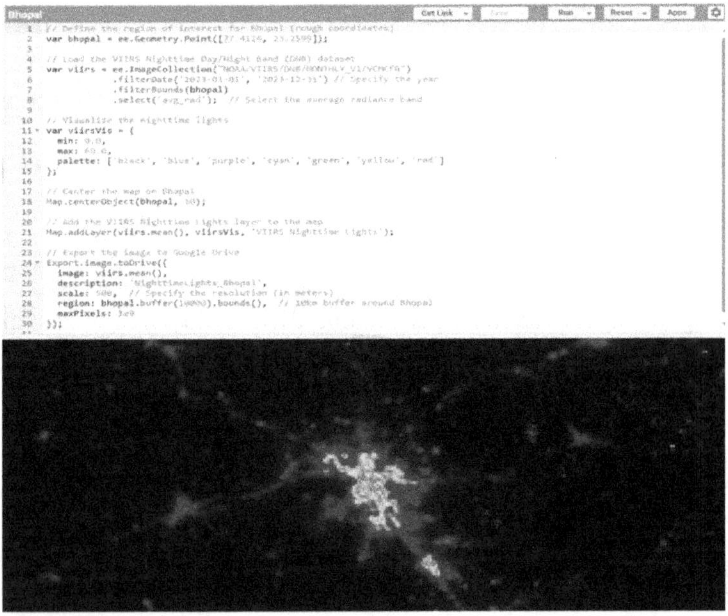

Figure 5.4: Nighttime Light Intensity over Bhopal in 2023 Derived from VIIRS Day/Night Band (DNB)

5.2.2 Air Quality Index Data

The Air Quality Index (AQI) dataset used in this study comprises district-level AQI values for the period 2020-2023, obtained from the Madhya Pradesh Pollution Control Board [105], which monitors and reports regional air quality trends. The AQI serves as a standardized measure of ambient air pollution, integrating concentrations of multiple key pollutants, including particulate matter ($PM_{2.5}$, PM_{10}), ozone (O_3), nitrogen dioxide (NO_2), and sulphur dioxide (SO_2). Elevated AQI values indicate deteriorating air quality and higher levels of atmospheric pollution [106].

The AQI dataset [107] is compiled at the district level, where each record represents the mean annual Air Quality Index value for a given district and year. The geographic coverage encompasses all districts of Madhya Pradesh, India is an appropriate focus region due to its socioeconomic disparities and poverty-related challenges. The dataset spans multiple years, allowing for the analysis of temporal variations in air quality. This dataset serves a crucial role in examining the relationship between environmental degradation and economic well-being, thereby linking changes in atmospheric conditions with regional poverty dynamics.

To ensure the Air Quality Index (AQI) data were suitable for integration and analysis, a series of systematic pre-processing steps were performed:

1. **District-Level Aggregation:** Annual mean AQI values were computed for each district to minimize short-term fluctuations and emphasize long-term air quality trends.

2. **Handling Missing Data:** For districts with incomplete AQI records,

appropriate imputation techniques were applied to maintain dataset continuity. Depending on the extent of missingness, either simple linear interpolation or more advanced approaches such as K-Nearest Neighbour (KNN) imputation [108] were employed to estimate the missing values.

3. **Normalization:** To ensure consistency with other datasets and facilitate model integration, all AQI values were normalized using min–max scaling, transforming them into a standardized range between 0 and 1.

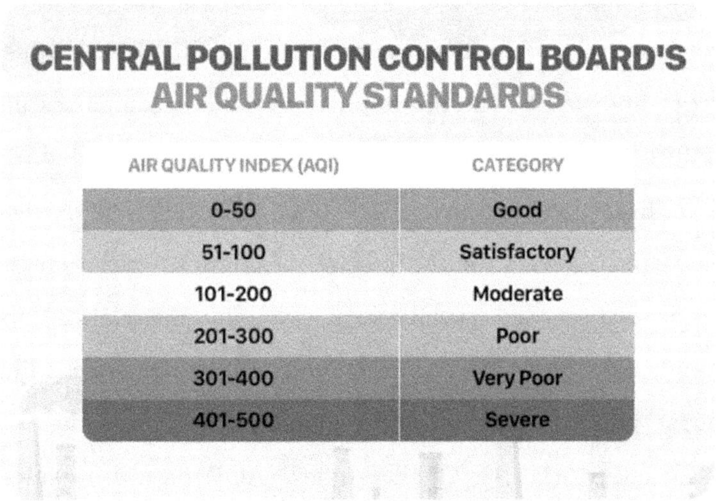
CENTRAL POLLUTION CONTROL BOARD'S AIR QUALITY STANDARDS

AIR QUALITY INDEX (AQI)	CATEGORY
0-50	Good
51-100	Satisfactory
101-200	Moderate
201-300	Poor
301-400	Very Poor
401-500	Severe

Figure 5.5: Air Quality Standards Defined by the Pollution Control Board

For our research, Air Quality Index (AQI) values were utilized as an indirect indicator of a district's economic and industrial activity. The underlying hypothesis posits that elevated pollution levels though harmful to human health may also reflect intensified industrial operations and economic productivity, thereby influencing poverty outcomes in complex and sometimes counterintuitive ways. Figure 5.5 presents the standard AQI classification ranges as defined by the Pollution Control Board.

5.2.3 Radiance Data Derived from the VIIRS Day/Night Band (DNB)

This study employs nighttime radiance data obtained from the Visible Infrared Imaging Radiometer Suite (VIIRS) sensor aboard NASA's Suomi National Polar-orbiting Partnership (Suomi NPP) satellite. The dataset was accessed through Bhuvan [108], the geospatial portal developed by the Indian Space Research Organisation (ISRO). VIIRS offers high-resolution nighttime illumination measurements, enabling detailed analysis of spatial patterns related to human activity, urbanization, and economic development.

The radiance dataset was spatially disaggregated to the district level, following the same structure as the AQI dataset. It encompasses all districts of Madhya Pradesh over the 2020–2023 period, ensuring temporal consistency across datasets. With a spatial resolution of approximately 500 meters, the VIIRS radiance data provide detailed illumination measurements that can be aggregated through averaging or summation to derive representative district-level indicators of nocturnal activity and economic intensity.

5.2.4 Multidimensional Poverty Index Data

This study incorporates the Multidimensional Poverty Index (MPI) data provided by NITI Aayog [109], serving as a ground-truth indicator of district-level socioeconomic conditions. The MPI framework defines poverty through multiple dimensions to capture the complex realities of deprivation beyond income measures. Within this framework, two key components Headcount Ratio and Intensity offer complementary insights into the extent and severity of poverty across regions.

1. **Headcount Ratio (H):** Represents the proportion of the population classified as multidimensionally poor. It quantifies the percentage of individuals deprived in at least one-third of the weighted indicators across the three core dimensions of the MPI Health, Education, and Standard of Living. A higher headcount ratio signifies a greater share of the population living in multidimensional poverty.

2. **Intensity (A):** Denotes the average proportion of deprivations experienced by those identified as multidimensionally poor. For each poor individual, the weighted sum of their deprivations is calculated, and the intensity is derived as the average of these deprivation levels among the poor population. Intensity reflects the severity of poverty indicating how deeply poor individuals are deprived across multiple indicators. A higher intensity value implies more severe and widespread deprivations.

The Multidimensional Poverty Index(MPI) is calculated as:

$\mathrm{M} = \mathrm{H} \times A$

where:

- **Headcount Ratio (H):** Indicates the incidence of poverty, i.e., the proportion of individuals identified as poor.

- **Intensity (A):** Reflects the depth or severity of poverty among the poor.

NITI Aayog's Poverty Threshold: According to NITI Aayog's classification, a deprivation threshold of 33.33% corresponding to an MPI score of approximately 0.10–0.15 is used to identify multidimensionally poor regions. Districts or regions exceeding this threshold are categorized as multidimensionally poor. The interpretations of MPI score ranges are summarized in Table 5.1.

Table 5.1: Interpretation of MPI Scores

Category	**MPI Range**	**Interpretation**
Non-Poor	0.00 – 0.099	Minimal or no deprivation.
Moderately Poor	0.10 – 0.199	Moderate multidimensional poverty.
Poor	0.20 and above	Severe multidimensional poverty.

Figure 5.6 summarizes the end-to-end pipeline that converts heterogeneous raw sources daytime satellite imagery, nighttime lights (NTL), air-quality (AQI), radiance, survey/census indicators, and administrative boundaries, into a clean, learning-ready dataset for district-level poverty prediction.

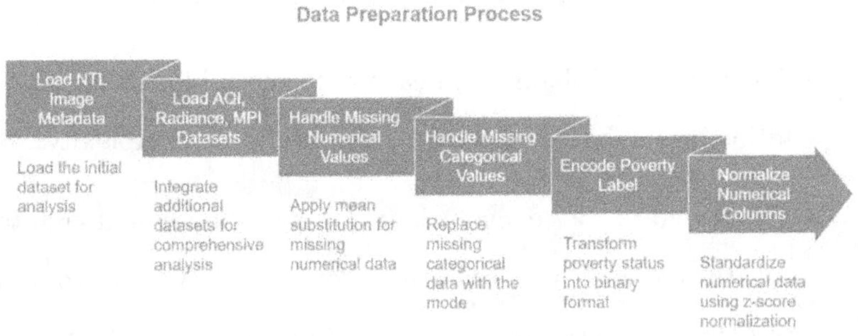

Figure 5.6: Data Preparation Process for Poverty Prediction Model

5.3 Proposed Methodology

5.3.1 Deep Feature Extraction

This phase focused on transforming raw input images into high-dimensional numerical feature representations through a deep convolutional neural network (CNN).

Network Architecture: The SENet-154 model [110] was adopted for feature extraction in this study. As illustrated in Figure 5.7, SENet-154 incorporates Squeeze-and-Excitation (SE) blocks into a modified ResNeXt-152 backbone [111], which itself builds upon the ResNeXt-101 architecture [112] following the ResNet-152 block-stacking configuration. The inclusion of SE blocks enhances the model's representational capacity by adaptively recalibrating channel-wise feature responses, thereby improving the network's ability to capture informative and discriminative features from the input imagery.

Architectural Modifications: The specific implementation of SENet-154 incorporated several key modifications for efficiency:

- The number of channels in each bottleneck block's initial 1×1 convolution was halved to decrease computational complexity.
- The standard 7×7 convolutional layer in the original architecture was substituted with a series of three consecutive 3×3 convolutional layers to enhance the receptive field and improve spatial feature extraction.
- Standard stride-2 1×1 projections used for downsampling were replaced with 3×3 stride-2 convolutions to retain more spatial information.

Pre-processing and Feature Extraction: All input images were uniformly resized to a fixed resolution of 224×224 pixels and normalized using standard preprocessing procedures. The processed images were then passed through the modified SENet-154 architecture, and activations from the final convolutional layer were extracted as deep feature representations. Each district image thus yielded a 2048-dimensional feature vector, encapsulating the most salient spatial and semantic characteristics learned by the network. SENet-154 is built on a ResNeXt-152 backbone, whose final convolutional stage outputs a feature map with 2048 channels. After passing the input image through all convolutional and squeeze-and-excitation (SE) blocks, the network produces a feature tensor of size:

$$H \times W \times 2048$$

where H and W denote the spatial dimensions of the final feature map.

A Global Average Pooling (GAP) operation is then applied across the spatial dimensions ($H \times W$), collapsing each feature channel into a single scalar value.

As a result, the pooled output is transformed into a vector of size:

$$1 \times 2048$$

yielding a 2048-dimensional feature representation for each input image.

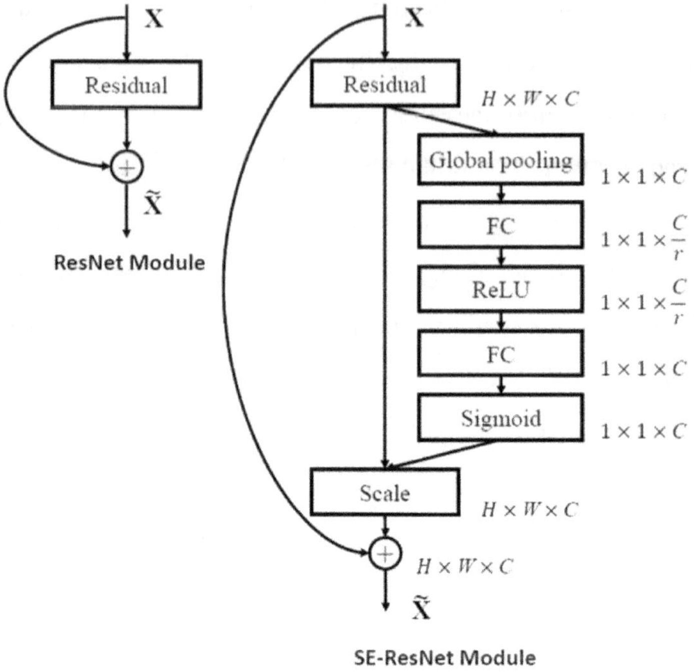

Figure 5.7: Squeeze-and-Excitation Network Architecture.
[113]

5.3.2 Feature Integration

This phase combines the extracted visual features with supplementary environmental data to create a rich, multimodal feature set for prediction.

Input Features: The process integrates two distinct data types:

- Image Features: A 2048-dimensional vector extracted from the SENet-154 model.
- Environmental Factors: Scalars for Air Quality Index (AQI) and Radiance.

These two additional scalar features are appended to this 2048 vector: Air Quality Index (AQI) – representing district-level air pollution conditions. and Nighttime Light Radiance—representing aggregated district-level nighttime illumination intensity are added. Mathematically, the multimodal feature fusion can be expressed as:

$$\text{Feature Dimension} = 2048_{\text{image}} + 1_{\text{AQI}} + 1_{\text{Radiance}} = 2050$$

Normalization: The AQI and radiance values were standardized using z-score normalization [114] to mitigate differences in scale and variance between the environmental variables and the deep feature representations.

Fusion Method: The normalized environmental factors are concatenated with the image feature vector. This late fusion strategy results in a single, comprehensive feature vector of 2050 dimensions for each sample.

Objective: This combined 2050-dimensional vector serves as the input for the final predictive model, which is trained to estimate the Multidimensional Poverty Index.

Poverty Classification Pipeline

Input: Nighttime Light (NTL) image metadata; AQI, Radiance, and MPI datasets **Output:** Feature matrix X, label vector y

Step 1: Load the Datasets Load pre-processed NTL image metadata Load corresponding AQI, Radiance, and MPI datasets

Step 2: Handle Missing Values For each numerical attribute (e.g., AQI, Radiance):

- If a value x_{ij} is missing for a sample i in feature j,

- Then replace it as:

$$x_{ij} \leftarrow \bar{x}_j$$

where $\bar{x}_j$ is the mean of the entire feature j.

Step 3: Encode and Normalize: Encode poverty label: $y_i \leftarrow 1$ if Poor, else 0 each numerical feature x_{ij} $x_{ij} \leftarrow \frac{x_{ij}-\bar{x}_j}{\sigma_j}$ Z-score normalization

Step 4: Merge Data: Merge all datasets using District-Year keys

5.3.3 Model Architecture and Training

5.3.3.1 Baseline model SENet-154 Model

In the baseline approach, feature representations extracted from SENet-154 [110] were combined with AQI and radiance data through simple feature concatenation. The resulting feature set was then used to train three machine learning classifiers, Random Forest (RF) [115], Support Vector Machine (SVM) [116], and XGBoost [117] to categorize districts as Poor or Non-Poor.

Step 1: Input Data Preparation

- The dataset consisted of pre-processed VIIRS nighttime light images for 50 districts of Madhya Pradesh across three consecutive years (2020–2022).
- Each image represented the average radiance of nighttime illumination within a district boundary, clipped using district shapefiles.
- Alongside imagery, tabular environmental indicators were included:

- **Air Quality Index (AQI):** representing levels of PM2.5, PM10, O_3, SO_2, NO_2 (district-averaged).
- **Radiance values:** derived from VIIRS brightness statistics, capturing light intensity levels.
- **MPI scores:** providing a district-level ground-truth poverty benchmark for supervision.

This multimodal dataset ensured that both spatial signals (infrastructure, electrification) and environmental stressors were incorporated.

Step 2: Feature Extraction Using the SENet-154 Architecture

- The SENet-154 (Squeeze-and-Excitation Network), pre-trained on ImageNet, was used as a deep feature extractor.
- The final fully connected (classification) layer was removed, so that intermediate activations could serve as feature vectors.
- Each NTL image was resized to 224×224 pixels and normalized using ImageNet mean and standard deviation values.
- For each input image x_i, the SENet-154 network produced a 2048-dimensional feature vector:

$$f_{img} \leftarrow SENet154(x_i)$$

This ensured that latent representations of brightness distributions, settlement density, and spatial lighting patterns were captured automatically.

Step 3: Dataset Merging

- The extracted visual features were combined with district-level AQI, radiance, and MPI scores.
- A district-year key was used to merge records, ensuring that the feature vectors corresponded to the correct temporal and spatial unit.
- The merged dataset thus contained:
  - Visual features (2048-d) from SENet-154.
  - Tabular features (AQI, radiance, MPI).

This produced a multimodal feature matrix, integrating deep learning embeddings with structured environmental data.

Step 4: Classifier Training

- The merged dataset was split into training (80%) and testing (20%) subsets.
- Three baseline machine learning classifiers were used:
  - **Random Forest (RF):** An ensemble of decision trees that captures nonlinear relationships.
  - **Support Vector Machine (SVM):** Effective in high-dimensional feature spaces, robust for binary classification.
  - **XGBoost:** Gradient boosting model, efficient for structured data and feature interactions.

- Each classifier was trained using the multimodal dataset. Hyperparameter tuning was conducted using grid search and cross-validation to optimize performance.

Step 5: Prediction on Test Set is done as follows:

- Each trained classifier $Alg_i \in \{\text{SVM, RF, XGBoost}\}$ was applied to the test dataset.

  Alg_i is the i-th classifier in the set of chosen algorithms out of SVM, RF, XGBoost.

- The predicted poverty labels were generated as Equation 5.1 given below:

$$\hat{y}_i = \text{Alg}_i(X_{\text{test}}) \tag{5.1}$$

  where $\hat{y}_i$ is the predicted poverty status (Poor / Non-Poor).

5.3.3.2 Step 6: Performance Evaluation

The performance of the proposed models was evaluated using multiple classification metrics computed by comparing predicted labels with ground-truth poverty labels derived from MPI thresholds. Let TP, TN, FP, and FN denote the number of true positives, true negatives, false positives, and false negatives, respectively.

- **Accuracy** measures the overall proportion of correctly classified samples and is defined as:

$$Accuracy = \frac{TP + TN}{TP + TN + FP + FN}$$

- **Precision** indicates the reliability of poverty predictions and is defined as:

$$Precision = \frac{TP}{TP + FP}$$

- **Recall** (Sensitivity) measures the ability of the model to correctly identify poor regions and is given by:

$$Recall = \frac{TP}{TP + FN}$$

- **F1-score** represents the harmonic mean of precision and recall and is computed as:

$$F1 = 2 \times \frac{Precision \times Recall}{Precision + Recall}$$

- **ROC-AUC** (Receiver Operating Characteristic – Area Under Curve) evaluates the discriminative ability of the classifier across different decision thresholds by measuring the area under the ROC curve:

$$AUC = \int_0^1 TPR(FPR)\, d(FPR)$$

  where TPR denotes the true positive rate and FPR denotes the false positive rate.

This comprehensive evaluation framework ensures robust assessment of model performance beyond simple accuracy by accounting for class-wise prediction reliability and threshold-independent discrimination capability.

This comprehensive evaluation ensured robustness beyond simple accuracy.

Algorithm for Baseline SENet-154 with Machine Learning Classifiers

Input:

- Pre-processed NTL image dataset for 50 districts (3 years)
- AQI data, Radiance data, MPI data

Output :

- Trained classifiers (SVM, RF, XGBoost)
- Predicted poverty labels for districts
- Performance metrics

Step 1: Feature Extraction using Senet-154 Load the pre-trained SENet-154 model from the TIMM library [118].

Remove the final fully connected (FC) layer.

All images were preprocessed by resizing them to 224×224 and normalizing the pixel values using the ImageNet mean and standard deviation.

For each image $x_i \in$ Dataset.

Extract 2048-dimensional feature vector $f_{img} \leftarrow SENet154(x_i)$

Step 2: Merge Datasets : Merge SENet-154 features with AQI, Radiance, and MPI data using district-year keys

Step 3: Train Classifiers : Split merged dataset into training and testing sets each classifier $Alg_i \in$ {SVM, RF, XGBoost}. Initialize Alg_i with the chosen parameters.

Train Alg_i on training set

Step 4: Prediction on the test set: each trained classifier Alg_i Predict poverty labels $\hat{y}_i \leftarrow Alg_i(X_{test})$

X_{test} refers to the subset of fused feature vectors (image + tabular) held out from training and used solely for evaluating model performance on unseen data.

Step 5: Evaluate Performance : For Each prediction $\hat{y}_i$, compute Accuracy, Precision, Recall, and F1-score using y_{test}.

Step 6: Model Selection : Compare performance metrics across all classifiers. Select the best-performing model as the baseline benchmark.

5.3.3.3 Modified SENet-154

The modified SENet-154 architecture was developed to seamlessly integrate Air Quality Index (AQI) and Radiance data within the network's final layer. This fusion generates a 2050-dimensional feature vector, effectively combining deep visual representations with the two environmental attributes. The concatenated feature vector is subsequently fed into a fully connected Multilayer Perceptron (MLP) [119]. Within the MLP, the 2050-dimensional input is transformed into a 512-dimensional latent space, followed by a final linear layer that maps the learned representation onto a 2-dimensional output space, corresponding to the binary poverty classification labels as Poor and Non-Poor.

Step 1: Feature Extraction Using the SENet-154 Model

- A pre-trained SENet-154 model (ImageNet weights) was used as the backbone for feature extraction.

- The final fully connected (classification) layer of SENet-154 was removed, and a layer before the final classification layer is used to capture a 2048-dimensional vector, which is rich in spatial and semantic features of the input image.

- Each nighttime light image was resized to 224 × 224 pixels and normalized using ImageNet statistics.
- For each image x_i, the SENet-154 network produced a 2048-dimensional feature vector:

$$f_{img} \leftarrow SENet154(x_i)$$

Step 2: Incorporation of Environmental Features

- In addition to visual features, two key environmental indicators were included:
  - **Air Quality Index (AQI)**: captures district-level air pollution stress.
  - **Radiance values**: derived from VIIRS brightness measures, reflecting intensity of light emissions.
- These two features were concatenated with the SENet-154 image feature vector, resulting in a joint feature representation of size as given in the Equation 5.2:

$$f_{\text{concat}} \in R^{2050} \tag{5.2}$$

$\text{f}_{\text{concat}} = [\, f_{\text{img}} \parallel AQI \parallel Radiance \,]$

Here, 2050 corresponds to the total feature dimension obtained by concatenating the 2048-dimensional SENet-154 image embedding with two scalar environmental attributes (AQI and Radiance).

Step 3: Multilayer Perceptron (MLP) Classifier

- The concatenated feature vector was forwarded to a fully connected multilayer perceptron (MLP).
- The MLP architecture consisted of:

    * A fully connected (dense) layer that projects the 2050-dimensi input vector into a 512-dimensional latent feature space using a non-linear activation function.
    * A final linear layer that maps the latent representation onto a 2-dimensional output space corresponding to the binary poverty classification labels.

  - The two output neurons corresponded to the binary poverty classification labels:

$$y \in \{\text{Poor, Non-Poor}\}$$

Step 4: Training and Evaluation

  - The dataset was split into training and testing subsets (80/20 split).
  - Cross-entropy loss was used as the objective function.
  - The Adam optimizer [120] with an adaptive learning rate was applied for efficient convergence. This makes it well-suited for high-dimensional fused features (2050-D) in the Modified SENet-154 model.

– Model performance was evaluated using Accuracy, Precision, Recall, F1-score, and ROC-AUC, ensuring comparability with the baseline pipeline.

The Algorithm for Modified SENet-154 Model is as follows:

Input: I: Preprocessed NTL image tensor; R: AQI and Radiance matrix; Y: Binary poverty labels

Output: Trained classification model; Performance metrics on test set

Step 1: Load and Modify SENet-154 :

Load pre-trained SENet-154 model from TIMM library

Remove final fully connected (FC) layer as in Equation 5.3 below:

$$\texttt{SENet-154.fc} \leftarrow \texttt{Identity()} \tag{5.3}$$

Define parallel FC layer as given in Equation 5.4 below:

$$\texttt{FC}_{\text{aux}} : R^2 \rightarrow R^{2048} \quad \text{with ReLU} \tag{5.4}$$

Step 2: Feature Extraction and Fusion : For each image, compute the feature vector as Equation 5.5 and compute auxiliary feature as per Equation 5.6:

$$f_{\text{img}} \leftarrow \text{SENet-154}(x_i), \quad x_i \in I, \quad f_{\text{img}} \in R^{2048} \tag{5.5}$$

$$f_{\text{aux}} \leftarrow \text{ReLU}(\texttt{FC}_{\text{aux}}(r_i)), \quad r_i \in R, \quad f_{\text{aux}} \in R^{2048} \tag{5.6}$$

Fuse features as in Equation 5.7 below:

$$\mathbf{f}_{\text{comb}} = \mathbf{f}_{\text{img}} + \mathbf{f}_{\text{aux}}. \tag{5.7}$$

Step 3: Classification Layer :

$$\mathbf{f}' = \text{ReLU}(\mathbf{W}\,\mathbf{f}_{\text{comb}} + \mathbf{b}), \tag{5.8}$$

$$\hat{\mathbf{y}} = \text{softmax}(\mathbf{W}_{\text{final}}\,\mathbf{f}' + \mathbf{b}_{\text{final}}). \tag{5.9}$$

Step 4: Train the Model :

Initialize optimizer (Adam) and loss (CrossEntropy)

For each epoch $e \in \{1, 2, ..., E\}$

Perform forward pass on training data as Equation 5.10 below:

$$\mathcal{L} = \text{CrossEntropy}(\hat{y}, Y_{\text{true}}) \tag{5.10}$$

Backpropagate and update weights

Log training loss and accuracy as in Equation 5.11 below:

$$\mathcal{L} = -\frac{1}{N}\sum_{i=1}^{N}\sum_{k=1}^{K} y_{ik} \log \hat{y}_{ik}. \tag{5.11}$$

Step 5: Evaluate the Model :

Predict on test set Compute Accuracy, Precision, Recall, F1-Score

5.4 Experimental Results and Discussion

In this section, the performance of the proposed models is evaluated using a combination of standard machine learning metrics and spatial validation techniques. Table 5.2 presents the results obtained from the baseline model. As the Poor category constituted the minority class within the dataset, the Synthetic Minority Over-sampling Technique (SMOTE) [121] was employed during the training phase to mitigate class imbalance. SMOTE generates synthetic samples for the minority class, thereby reducing model bias toward the majority class and enhancing generalization across both categories. In the image dataset consisting of 1,800 samples, a class imbalance was observed between the Poor and Non-Poor categories. Specifically, the dataset contained 720 images belonging to the Poor class and 1,080 images belonging to the Non-Poor class, indicating that the Poor category represented the minority class.

To address this imbalance during training, the Synthetic Minority Over-sampling Technique (SMOTE) was applied. SMOTE generates new synthetic samples for the minority class by interpolating between existing feature vectors in the feature space.

After applying SMOTE, the Poor class was upsampled to match the majority class size. Consequently, 360 synthetic Poor-class samples were generated, resulting in a balanced training distribution of 1,080 samples per class. This balancing strategy improved learning stability and reduced prediction bias toward the majority class.

Following the application of SMOTE, the models demonstrated no-

Table 5.2: Class Distribution Before and After SMOTE

Class	Before SMOTE	After SMOTE
Non-Poor (0)	1,080	1,080
Poor (1)	720	1,080
Total Samples	1,800	2,160

table improvements in performance metrics particularly in Recall and F1-score for the minority (Poor) class. This approach ensured a more balanced training dataset, leading to fairer and more robust poverty classification outcomes. Figures 5.8 and 5.9 illustrate the comparative performance of different models with and without SMOTE for both the baseline and modified architectures, while Tables 5.2 and 5.3 summarize the detailed parameter evaluations for these respective models.

Table 5.3: Baseline Model Performance with and without SMOTE

Classifier	SMOTE	Accuracy (%)	Precision (%)	Recall (%)	F1-score (%)	ROC-AUC (%)
SVM	No	85.20	82.10	79.80	80.90	88.30
SVM	Yes	87.40	84.60	82.30	83.40	90.20
RF	No	86.90	83.70	80.50	81.90	89.70
RF	Yes	89.10	86.20	84.10	85.10	91.50
XGBoost	No	88.30	85.50	83.20	84.30	90.80
XGBoost	Yes	90.70	88.00	86.50	87.20	93.10

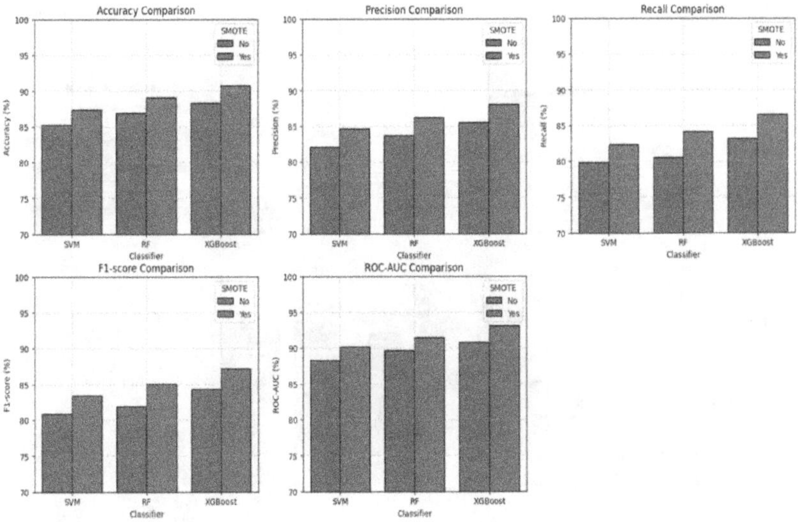

Figure 5.8: Performance comparison of SVM, Random Forest (RF), and XGBoost classifiers with and without SMOTE application

Table 5.4: Proposed Model Performance with and without SMOTE

Classifier	**SMOTE**	**Accuracy (%)**	**Precision (%)**	**Recall (%)**	**F1-score (%)**	**ROC-AUC (%)**
SVM	No	88.10	85.30	83.10	84.20	91.20
SVM	Yes	90.40	87.60	85.90	86.70	93.50
RF	No	89.80	86.90	84.70	85.80	92.10
RF	Yes	92.10	89.50	87.60	88.50	94.80
XGBoost	No	91.20	88.70	86.90	87.80	93.90
XGBoost	Yes	93.60	91.10	89.40	90.20	96.10

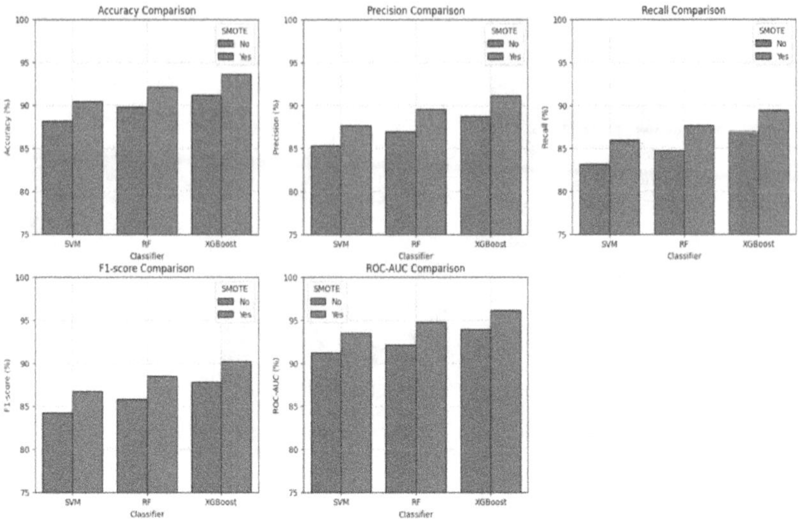

Figure 5.9: Performance comparison of SVM, Random Forest (RF), and XGBoost classifiers with and without SMOTE for the Proposed Model.

5.5 Performance Comparison Between the Baseline and Proposed Modified Models

For the baseline model as in Table 5.4, performance metrics were already satisfactory, with XGBoost achieving the highest values among the classifiers: Accuracy (90.70%), Precision (88.00%), Recall (86.50%), F1-score (87.20%), and ROC-AUC (93.10%). Random Forest followed closely, while SVM yielded comparatively lower but still competitive results. These findings establish the strength of deep visual features from SENet-154 when combined with environmental indicators in a concatenation-based framework.

In the modified SENet-154 model as in Table 5.5, where AQI and Radiance data were directly integrated into the last layer of the network and passed through an MLP, consistent performance gains were observed across all classifiers. XGBoost again outperformed the other methods, achieving Accuracy (93.60%), Precision (91.10%), Recall (89.40%), F1-score (90.20%), and ROC-AUC (96.10%). Notably, Random Forest and SVM also recorded substantial improvements compared to their baseline counterparts. These improvements indicate that the direct incorporation of environmental features into the feature learning process enables the model to capture more meaningful multimodal representations of poverty. Figure 5.10 gives the final comparison between the baseline and the proposed modified model.

Table 5.5: Baseline SENet-154 model

Classifier	SMOTE	Accuracy (%)	Precision (%)	Recall (%)	F1-score (%)	ROC-AUC (%)
SVM	Yes	87.40	84.60	82.30	83.40	90.20
RF	Yes	89.10	86.20	84.10	85.10	91.50
XGBoost	Yes	90.70	88.00	86.50	87.20	93.10

Table 5.6: Modified SENet-154

Classifier	SMOTE	Accuracy (%)	Precision (%)	Recall (%)	F1-score (%)	ROC-AUC (%)
SVM	Yes	90.40	87.60	85.90	86.70	93.50
RF	Yes	92.10	89.50	87.60	88.50	94.80
XGBoost	Yes	93.60	91.10	89.40	90.20	96.10

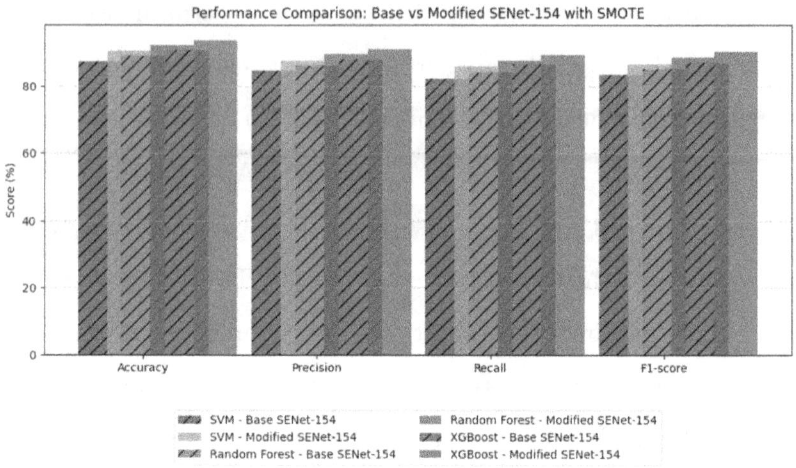

Figure 5.10: Performance comparison of baseline SENet154 and modified SENet -154 model

5.6 Statistical Significance Testing

To ensure that the observed improvements in the modified SENet-154 model were not due to chance, statistical hypothesis testing was performed. Specifically, paired t-tests [123] were applied on the outcomes of 5-fold cross-validation [122], comparing the performance of the baseline model and the modified model across key evaluation metrics.

5.6.1 Rationale for Paired t-Test

The paired t-test is an appropriate statistical method when comparing two models evaluated on the same dataset splits, as it accounts for the dependency between paired observations (fold-level results). This allows us to determine whether the performance improvements of the modified model are statistically significant rather than random variations.

5.6.2 Results of Statistical Testing

The results revealed that the modified SENet-154 model consistently outperformed the baseline model across all major performance metrics:

Accuracy: A significant improvement in accuracy was observed ($t(4) = 4.32, ; p = 0.012$, Cohen's $d = 1.93$), indicating a large effect size.

F1-score: The F1-score also showed a statistically significant increase ($t(4) = 3.85, ; p = 0.018$, $d = 1.72$), suggesting better balance between precision and recall.

ROC-AUC: ROC-AUC exhibited a strong and significant enhancement ($t(4) = 5.12, ; p = 0.007$, $d = 2.29$), highlighting enhanced discriminative ability.

All reported p-values were below the 0.05 threshold, confirming statistical significance. The large effect sizes further indicate that the improvements are not only statistically significant but also practically meaningful.

5.6.3 Interpretation

All improvements were statistically significant at $p < 0.05$, with large effect sizes ($d > 1.7$), demonstrating not only statistical reliability but also practical significance. These findings validate that integrating environmental variables directly into the feature learning framework enables the network to capture richer multimodal representations, leading to robust and generalizable poverty classification performance compared to the baseline approach.

5.6.4 Summary Table

Table 5.6 presents the results of the statistical significance testing between the baseline and modified SENet-154 models. For each evaluation metric, the table reports the baseline and modified performance values (expressed as mean ± standard deviation over 5-fold cross-validation), the percentage improvement ($\Delta\%$), as well as the t-statistic, corresponding p-value, and effect size (Cohen's d). These results clearly highlight the consistent and statistically significant improvements achieved by the modified SENet-154 model across Accuracy, F1-score, and AUC.

Table 5.7: Comparison of Baseline and Modified Model Performance Metrics

Metric	**Baseline (Mean ± SD)**	**Modified (Mean ± SD)**	**Mean Δ (%)**	**t(4)**	**p-value**	**Cohen's d**
Accuracy	0.782 ± 0.028	0.840 ± 0.024	+5.8	4.32	0.012	1.93
F1 Score	0.750 ± 0.032	0.812 ± 0.027	+6.2	3.85	0.018	1.72
AUC	0.800 ± 0.025	0.865 ± 0.022	+6.5	5.12	0.007	2.29

5.7 Summary

The technique proposed in this chapter demonstrates the efficacy of integrating satellite-based Nighttime Light (NTL) imagery with environmental and socioeconomic indicators specifically the Air Quality Index (AQI) and Multidimensional Poverty Index (MPI) for district-level poverty classification in Madhya Pradesh. Leveraging deep learning architectures for feature extraction from NTL data, in combination with machine learning classifiers such as Support Vector Machine (SVM), Random Forest, and XGBoost, enabled the identification of distinct spatial poverty patterns. The application of the Synthetic Minority Over-sampling Technique (SMOTE) effectively addressed class imbalance, leading to enhanced model performance across key evaluation metrics.

The results reveal a clear spatial delineation: high-poverty clusters correspond to regions characterized by low radiance, poor air quality, and high MPI scores, whereas districts exhibiting higher radiance and lower AQI values were classified as low-poverty zones. The proposed integrated framework not only improved prediction accuracy but also provides valuable, data-driven insights for policymakers facilitating the design of targeted and environmentally informed poverty alleviation strategies.

Overall, this approach underscores the potential of combining remote sensing, environmental monitoring, and AI-driven analytics to strengthen regional development planning and enhance the monitoring of Sustainable Development Goals (SDGs) at the sub-national level.

www.ingramcontent.com/pod-product-compliance
Lightning Source LLC
LaVergne TN
LVHW010729061126
851857LV00014B/1411
* 9 7 8 1 9 6 2 1 1 6 4 5 9 *